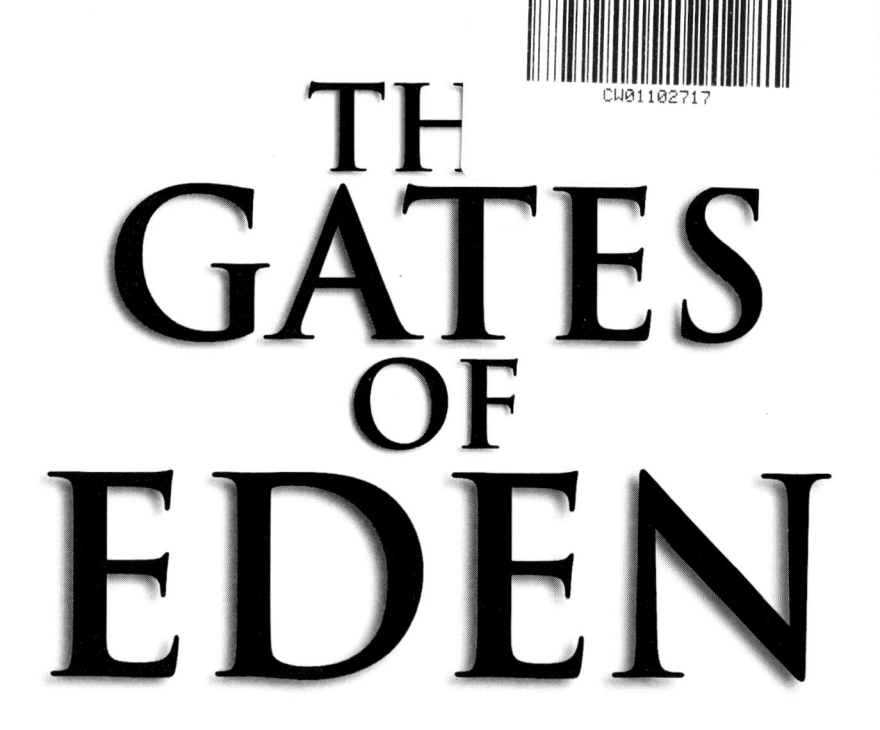

# THE GATES OF EDEN

**Vance Royal Olson**

THE GATES OF EDEN copyright © 2015 Vance Royal Olson
All rights reserved.

ISBN: 978-0-9931299-2-6

*Published by:*
The Blacksmith Arms Publishing House
London, England

*Print design and cover layout:*
Simona Meloni

*email:*
blacksmithpublishing@gmail.com

# TABLE OF CONTENTS

Preface ........................................................................... 7
Excerpts from *The Road to Eden* ............................................ 11
   A Twilight Encounter ....................................................... 11
   The Hydraulics of an Open Heaven .................................. 16
Chapter 1 - The Father's Love: Gate of Heaven .................... 19
Chapter 2 - Beginnings: Wisdom Calls from the Gates ......... 27
   First Answers ................................................................... 27
   Overcoming Fear .............................................................. 30
   Pressure ............................................................................ 33
   Training and Commissioning ........................................... 37
Chapter 3 - The London Scene: Gates of the City ................. 41
   Ichthus House ................................................................... 42
   The Dietrich Bonhoeffer Memorial Church .................... 48
   The New Life Centre ......................................................... 51
   Number 7 Combedale Road ............................................. 58
   The Haunted House on Beaconsfield Road .................... 60
Chapter 4 - God's Hydraulics and the Right of Access: Gates of the Earth .................................................................. 67
   Discernment and the Key of Knowledge .......................... 68
   Access: Using the Key of Knowledge ............................... 72
   Unbelief ............................................................................. 78
   Spiritualism ...................................................................... 80

  Slavery .................................................................... 81
  Fashion .................................................................. 81
  Architecture ......................................................... 85
  Music .................................................................... 88
  Philosophy and Academia: John Wycliffe ...................... 89
  A Note of Caution ................................................ 94
Chapter 5 - WWII and the Cross: Gate of Hope and Glory ... 97
  An Old Desire ....................................................... 97
  Ron ..................................................................... 101
  Brian and the Gates of Hades ......................... 103
  The Quest for the Unified Field ...................... 107
  The Cross and the War ..................................... 109
Chapter 6 - Transtemporal Intercession: Gates of the Ages 113
  Moses, Paul and Israel's Destiny ..................... 115
  Indicators and Tokens ....................................... 119
Chapter 7 - Heart of Light: Breaking the Iron Gate of
  Religion ............................................................... 123
  Healer of Broken Hearts ................................... 123
  The Catholic Church ......................................... 125
  Mary Grace ......................................................... 126
  The Father at the Cross ..................................... 128
  Epilogue .............................................................. 131
Chapter 8 - The Church of England: Battle at the Gate ...... 135
  The Martyrdom of David Watson ................... 135
  St Paul's Cathedral ............................................. 137
  King Henry's Legacy .......................................... 143
  Queen Elizabeth's Oak ...................................... 146
  First Fruits .......................................................... 148

- Chapter 9 - Lord of the Whole Earth: Gate of the Peoples ... 151
  - Dialectic .................................................................... 151
  - Jerusalem: Gate of the Peoples ........................................ 154
  - Lord of all the Earth ....................................................... 156
  - The Church: Light of the World, Salt of the Earth ....... 160
  - A Surprising Observation .............................................. 161
- Chapter 10 - Travailing Desire: Entering the Gates ............. 165
- Appendix 1 - The Reality of Universals ................................ 173
  - Reality vs. Nominalism ................................................. 174
  - Understanding Universals ............................................. 181
  - The Human Body ......................................................... 186
  - Levels of Reality ........................................................... 187
  - The Interface of Spirit and Body ................................... 191
  - Universals and Creation ............................................... 196
  - On Quantum Theory .................................................... 200
- Appendix 2 - The Armour of Ghostly Battle ........................ 203

# Preface

In the first book in this series I told some of the stories of my youth and childhood, especially experiences of my father's love and how that became a doorway into the heavenly Father's love. *The Road to Eden* is the journey into knowing God our Father, as we were created to know him. This book takes up the story of what happened in the seven years that followed. I will begin with a short excerpt from the earlier book so that this one can stand alone if necessary.

'Gates' in the Bible is often a metaphor for the place of ruling and authority because the elders and governors of ancient cities assembled at the gates—'city hall' by modern parlance. Additionally, gates had a literal physical role in the military security of the city, and in being the place where trade and the movement of people could be controlled.

When Adam and Eve were expelled from the Garden of Eden, God placed at its gate behind them, '*...the Cherubim, and a flaming sword which turned every way, to guard the way to the tree of life.*' (Genesis 3:24) The Hebrew root concept relating to the word 'Cherubim' (which is not formally defined) suggests the idea of guarding and intercession—and with the flaming sword, we can add spiritual warfare. Before Jesus came, died, and rose again, however, we were on the wrong side of the gates, and the wrong end of the sword.

*'But to all who received him, who believed in his name, he gave power to become children of God.'* (John 1:12) We have been offered access in Christ, through the cross, to the authority of God our Father once again. And we are invited in the Lord's Prayer to exert that will and authority of God—his kingdom—on earth, by prayer and intercession; a work which takes us back to Adam and Eve's proper occupation, before they fell to sin. In sum: *The Gates of Eden* is about the place of intimacy, love, intercession and warfare through which the sons and daughters release their Father's will and kingdom on earth.

If you don't like the subjects of prayer, spiritual warfare and intercession—with all the strange mystical and spiritual talk that surrounds them—this is probably not the book for you. I make little effort to convince sceptics of anything; rather, I assume my readers are born again in the death and resurrection of Jesus, baptised in the Holy Spirit, and have at least rudimentary knowledge of those things of the Spirit which the Apostle Paul says are foolishness to worldly thinkers. (Ref: I Corinthians 2:14)

And finally, please remember what James said: *'...for we all make many mistakes.'* (James 3:2) This is my own story about a season of prayer as I understood it at the time, from memory, and with hindsight, but of course many details are left out. Then, too, many things that were only embryonic in 1984 are developed more fully here—I can't always remember exactly what I was thinking at that time. My prayer is that the Holy Spirit will guide you into his truth and cause any wrong or unhelpful words to fall by the wayside.

## Prologue

# Excerpts from *The Road to Eden*

*'See that you do not despise one of these little ones; for I tell you that in heaven their angels always behold the face of my Father who is in heaven.'*
(Jesus Christ, Matthew 18:10)

## A Twilight Encounter

*September, 1983*

I pressed my knees as best I could up against my CX500's V-twin engine for whatever scraps of warmth I could draw from it as it propelled me through the twilight toward the deepening gloom of night. The cheerful little engine seemed as oblivious to the darkness and the chill blowing in off the North Sea as to the last remnants of my slowly resolving frustration. Nor did the bleak, muddy flats of western Belgium, which were disappearing into the darkness, dampen its spirited diligence as we pushed mile after mile, first northward from Dunkirk, then westward toward Brussels.

I had always loved twilight, and my mind drifted back to an evening years earlier—a soft, warm evening when I was a child playing in the farmyard back home. Through an open window, I could hear my mum playing her piano and singing. The beauty of her worship flowing through the evening air caressed both soul and body and, merging with the interminable distances of the twilight, drew me into one deep undefined longing: joy-sorrow, as unexpected as ever.

A sudden extra chill in the air jolted me out of the remembrance, and I tried to tighten the bottom of my jacket around my waist. There was no question of stopping for the night—I only had enough money for fuel and food. I looked again across the shadowy landscape in the last light of that September evening and wondered at the barren, cold dampness of it. This was a different twilight and I thought of the battles that had been fought here in two world wars.

The grisly image of a young German soldier trying to gather up his intestines and put them back in his abdomen flashed across my mind. It was from stories told by my father's old friend, Bill Perrot, who had fought in the First World War when ammunition was in short supply and the fighting frequently reverted to knives and bayonets. Most of the soldiers never talked about what they had seen, but Bill was different (for reasons unknown) and this particular story had traversed a generation and was fixed in my imagination. I could even see the ghastly terror on the young German's face as the final blow was struck—ostensibly in kindness at that point, as the story went. My father hated war.

*The Gates of Eden*

My thoughts drifted back to the present day and my current situation. I would have been well into the warmer regions of central Germany by now if not for an annoying delay in getting out of London. Someone had asked me to wait outside a meeting he was in, then—forgetting me—exited the meeting by a different door, leaving me to wait 'patiently' for several hours. The plan for a leisurely late-morning departure had become an irritated rush mid afternoon. And because of that, I had left my gloves on the hall shelf—a fact which was now painfully presenting itself to me. How pleasant would those generous motorcycle gauntlets have been, I thought, as the cold, damp air found its way up my sleeves. Still, it was my own fault for being so grumpy when I left.

Then my mind began to wander down a path that it had never previously travelled. My hands were really very cold by now and I began to wonder if a person could ask God for something when it was his own fault that he didn't have it already, and when he could see no possible way for God to answer. After all, there didn't seem much chance of bumping into a generous Christian with an extra pair of gloves on this forsaken road—and I had no family on this continent, and not a penny to spare for extras. As I was reflecting on this theological point about prayer, but before I had a chance to pray—and I hadn't even decided if it would be appropriate to pray—two ancient-looking figures in black hooded capes, resembling the grim reaper, appeared about a metre in front of my hands, each holding a large block of ice. They hovered above the road and moved backwards, facing me, at the same speed as I was travelling. There would have been times that such apparitions would have terrified me, but on this occasion I simply thought, 'Humph, they've been there awhile and I just didn't see them.'

Then a memory began flooding across my mind of a day when I was about three or four years old and riding with my father on the tractor—a McCormick WD9, with no enclosure to shield the driver or his tagalongs from the elements. It was twilight, the temperature was dropping rapidly and we had probably another hour to go to finish the field. I remembered my boyish thoughts exactly: 'If I tell Dad I'm cold, he'll say, "I'd better take you into the house to Mum while I finish."' (The field was right next to the farmyard.) 'But... I want to stay with him... but my hands are freezing.'

I looked up into my dad's face, sort of trying to pretend I wasn't cold, but hoping for some help as well. I saw in his face the perfect understanding of my dilemma—he knew I didn't want to say I was cold and he knew why. And besides that, I could see that he was pleased that I wanted to be with him, and he was pleased to have me with him. This whole complex thought was held in one glimpse of his face in an instant: Love.

Then the memory merged with my present situation: as I saw that look on my father's face in my memory, I was seeing the same look on my heavenly Father's face now, in Belgium. Instantly my two hooded tormenters dropped to the road and disappeared beneath my feet behind me.

Back on the farm, my father had said, 'Put your hands on these hydraulic pipes.' As he said this, he gestured toward the hydraulic control valve that was bolted on to the fender of the tractor near where I was standing. Delicious heat from the high-pressure oil lines flowed into my cold hands as I did this, and our faces met again with smiles.

My heavenly Father, on the road in Belgium, then said, 'Put your hands on my hydraulic system—where my Spirit is moving under pressure.'

I understood this as the call to intercession, and the whole incident, though it took only a moment reveals the inner heart of all kingdom work. But Jesus answered them, '*My Father is working still, and I am working.*' (John 5:17) Our Father is out in the cold working, and he makes it possible for us to join him and be with him.

This is the first, the deepest and the greatest desire of the Holy Spirit. The Holy Spirit brings to our tangible experience, from the depths of the Father's heart, the desire to be with us. This desire to be with us goes right back to before the foundation of the world; it is the *reason* for the foundation of the world; it is the foundation of all foundations; it is absolute bedrock. The Father imagined us, just as a man or woman might imagine having a son or daughter; and having seen us in his heart's eye, he cannot rest until he has us tangibly with him. This desire is also called love.

*Vance Royal Olson*

# The Hydraulics of an Open Heaven

I was only a little warmer after that experience but I had a different heart about it and I spent the rest of the night praying for people who were cold. I won't say it was fun or easy but it was joyful work, in good company, and much came of it in future days and years.

Mid morning the next day I arrived at Bodenseehof, spent a good week with friends, and had plenty of time to rest before packing for the return journey—via Freiburg because I wanted to see an old friend whose family had a vineyard in a village nearby. After a morning ride from Lake Constance, through the Black Forest to Freiburg, and lunch with my friend, I got back on the road for the long drive to Dunkirk.

The forecast was for rain and already the sky was almost fully overcast as my CX500 crunched slowly through the loose stones of the vineyard's driveway to the village street. The sky ahead looked dark and foreboding, but there was still a slight break in the clouds where I was. Before long, the road was wet, and I expected to drive into rain at any moment. However, the rain was staying just ahead... and I began to think it was a bit odd. After about an hour, there was rain behind as well, then rain to one side, and then to the other side—but still none on me; always a little opening in the clouds.

This opening continued throughout the afternoon as I headed northward, up the Rhine Valley to Karlsruhe, and then Mannheim. At one point it was raining right up to the sides of the road on both sides, and almost as close front and back; at other times, the clear area was larger. There was always a little patch of open sky and sometimes even sunshine just over me, and I began to know it was in answer to my prayers for all cold people, on the outbound journey a week earlier. At Mannheim, the route was to take a sharp left toward Kaiserslautern and Luxembourg, and I wondered if the little bit of open sky would turn as well. It did.

The opening continued with me until nightfall when I decided to get a few hours' sleep in Luxembourg Airport—the one and only time I have used an airport as a free hotel. I drifted off to sleep, lying across some chairs and watching the heavy rain through the windows—pleased to be dry.

# CHAPTER 1

# THE FATHER'S LOVE: GATE OF HEAVEN

*But now in Christ Jesus you who were once far off have been brought near in the <u>blood of Christ</u>. For he is our peace, who has made us both one, and has broken down the dividing wall of hostility, by abolishing in his flesh the law of commandments and ordinances, that he might create in himself one new man in place of the two, so making peace, and might reconcile us both to God in one body <u>through the cross</u>, thereby bringing hostility to an end. And he came and preached peace to you who were far off and peace to those who were near; for through him we both have <u>access in one Spirit to the Father</u>'*
(Ephesians 2:13-18)

The central point and purpose of the Christian gospel is that human beings might have access to God the Father. Jesus lived in constant access to the Father, and his ministry on earth, his death, his resurrection, and the pouring out of his Spirit were all for the purpose of bringing human beings into that same relationship with the Father that he himself had.

The motivating and driving force behind the universe—the earth and all the heavens—is love: the great love of God the Father. Being the true Father, having seen us in his mind's eye and loved us before the foundation of the world, he took action—despite the great risk and cost—to have us. The truest and most beautiful words ever spoken to human ears must surely be those words of Jesus when he said: *'...the Father himself loves you...'* (John 16:27) These words answer the great 'why' of the universe and it is by the beauty and truth in these words that Jesus ordered his own life, even to death on the cross. There is no deeper motive; no agenda; no selfish wish; no need; no self-importance; no desire for power, fame, wealth or control, which lurks behind what Jesus and the Father did for us. At its deepest, the true gospel message is: God loves you. The Father himself loves you.

The personal encounter with the Father's love, recorded in the prologue, took place on the muddy flat land of western Belgium, 'Flanders Fields'; and the first fruit of the intercession, the miracle of an open sky above me as I rode the return trip a week later, took place in the Rhine valley and the road between Freiburg, Germany and Luxembourg. It is not surprising, therefore, that the main thrust of the warfare that followed concerned the roots and consequences of Nazi Germany and World War II. Of course these roots reach into the time before Hitler's political ascendancy and therefore also include the First World War as well as events, philosophies and theologies of the previous centuries.

Entangled, too, in those deep roots is the religious spirit with all its complex machinations. Hence several of my chapters concern warfare into the Catholic and the Anglican strongholds of religion. And of course my own journey involves overcoming the Lutheran stronghold. I'm not saying there isn't also a lot of good in each of these traditions, but only that every generation must retake or 're-understand' the basic truths of the gospel in the power of the Holy Spirit to overcome the power of the religious spirit which seems to creep into every organisation as time passes. Religious power arises from solidarities and agreements based on doing 'religious stuff' and talking 'religious talk' but not really knowing, loving and obeying Jesus. Doing 'religion' builds religious strongholds; but loving Jesus brings us into the Father's love. '... *For the Father himself loves you, because you have loved me and have believed that I came from the Father.'* (John 16:27)

Religious power—whether derived from corruptions of Christianity or the overtly false religions—is one of the four loveless powers by which the ancient serpent governs the fallen world. The other three powers are: military, political, and financial. Every evil and loveless event upon the earth flows from at least one of these powers; and the greatest evils of all are likely to flow from all four in conjunction. Matthew, for example, notes all four as complicit in the torture and murder of Jesus, as well as in resisting the resurrection, and witness to the resurrection. (Chapters 26-28)

In starkest contrast to these four loveless powers (which we could also call 'the world'), stands the love of the Father. John said: *'Do not love the world or the things in the world. If anyone loves the world, love for the Father is not in him.'* (I John 2:15) Jesus' love for the Father, expressed in his obedience to the Father, put him in direct conflict with the world—especially religious power—and we are certain to find the same. Of course, in the Father's love, Jesus overcame the world, and therefore in Him, we too can overcome.

The seven years of spiritual warfare that followed my commissioning in the Father's love reached fulfilment in 1991, a year to which many significant beginnings of change can be traced. I will note a few of these in later chapters, but perhaps most famously this is the year the Soviet era and cold war ended, the Berlin wall came down, and Germany was reunited.

For a period just after, almost everyone involved in spiritual warfare told stories of their part in the unexpected events of the early nineties. To this we should say, 'Praise God who is able to coordinate the resources of his church in a unified way, and who alone is the Lord of the Harvest with the overall strategy'. God clearly did involve many churches, organisations and individuals in ending the cold war peacefully. All that remains for us is to be humble and recognise that each one of his children is equally precious to him and each has an important and unique role to play in his grand scheme of things.

There's nothing wrong with feeling special in your work and ministry; the love of a true father heart will always make you feel like the favourite. Indeed, God has no sons or daughters who are not absolutely precious, special, unique and individually loved and treasured. Be sure to enjoy and savour that feeling, but also rejoice when any brothers or sisters feel the same—and always make every effort to ensure that anyone who doesn't feel special and precious also has their eyes opened to our heavenly Father's great love.

There are two things to be avoided here. First: false humility and dreary religious thinking to the effect that no one is special. Jesus said that even the least in the kingdom is greater than John the Baptist—and he seems pretty amazing and unique and special as far as I can see! Second: that we are 'more special' than our brothers and sisters. God's counsel to Cain makes it clear that our lives are not judged relative to those of our brothers or sisters. *'If you do well, will you not be accepted?'* (Genesis 4:7) Since we are each truly unique, we can only be judged against that blueprint and plan and destiny God had in his heart for us from the beginning. You are the only one who can be the perfect you. God loves you and wants you just as he uniquely chose you to be—he doesn't want you to be somebody else; he already has them. Therefore competition is an irrelevant and sinful distraction, which Cain, not heeding God's kind advice, fell tragically into.

Competition arises from selfish ambition and pride, the two greatest hindrances to spiritual warfare—the sins of Satan himself, and the foundation of the kingdom of darkness. Because of these two sins, many who start well end up fighting for the wrong side, and tragically, like the Pharisees, never realise it. As soon as our motivations become tainted with these sinful attitudes, we are disqualified because in so thinking we automatically turn away from the Father's face, the source of true authority.

The pure in heart see God according to Jesus, and that seeing is prerequisite to knowing our place, understanding our calling, and releasing the authority and power we have been given—indeed, it is actually *in* that 'seeing' that the power and authority are given. When we lose that sight of God the Father, we are tempted to copy techniques we have heard or read about. The root of this temptation is the desire to appear spiritual and successful; but of course giving in to it is certain to bring the opposite: failure, with the likely end of directly fighting our brothers and sisters on issues of position and honour—Cain and Abel, et al. ad nauseam.

The only legitimate way to engage in spiritual warfare is in the imitation of Jesus, led by the Holy Spirit, with our eyes on the Father's face. We get into that place by receiving his words of grace, resting and worshipping in them, and obeying the leadings of the Spirit. Imagining that we can 'fight' our way into such a place whenever we want is a snare even to those called and experienced in spiritual warfare; such is the treachery of pride. I'm afraid it's in that *'strive to enter that rest'* (Hebrews 4:11) range of paradoxes—not solvable by the mind alone. Rather, launch out into the deep and entrust yourself to the words of Jesus and to the Holy Spirit. Receive his love, like a child; and love him back, like a child.

*'Little children know the Father'* and *'Young men, strong in the word, fight and overcome the devil,'* John tells us in his first

letter. But—and it's a terribly big one I'm afraid—if we become 'jealous older brothers' instead of progressing and maturing into *'fathers who know Him who is from the beginning'* (I John 2:12-15) we have probably fallen into the snare of pride, because the 'fruit' always reveals the truth of our underlying motives. *'You will know them by their fruits.'* (Matthew 7:16)

The Father's love is both bedrock of beginning (little children knowing the Father), and distant star of destiny (fathers who *know* the eternal heavenly Father). Plainly stated, the true Gospel begins with the Father's love, and in that love it is also complete.

## CHAPTER 2
# BEGINNINGS: WISDOM CALLS FROM THE GATES

*'Does not wisdom call; does not understanding raise her voice? On the heights beside the way, in the path she takes her stand; beside the gates in front of the town, at the entrance of the portals she cries aloud: "To you, O men, I call, and my cry is to the sons of men."'*
(Proverbs 8: 1-4)

### FIRST ANSWERS

Before taking up the narrative in September, 1983 when I arrived back in London after the trip to Germany, I will go back to earlier times, starting with two examples of answered prayer in my childhood. The first was to do with frightening dreams when I was about five years old. They were recurring nightmares of being in an ancient cemetery that had stone boxes above ground. I had never seen such graves in my life, nor are any found in the vicinity of my childhood home on the prairies of western Canada—certainly none as old as in the dreams. Not until twenty years later, in London, England, did I see graves exactly as in those childhood terrors.

In the dreams, my brother was captured by ghosts who came up out of the graves and carried him down into the tunnels beneath. I knew in the dream that my brother had been taken to work in underground pepper factories and somehow the sensation of black pepper in my eyes and nose always accompanied the dream. Each time I had the dream, I went underground to rescue my brother but always ended up in terror and indecision at diverging tunnels before I got near him—and I could hear footsteps coming toward me from both tunnels. At that point I woke up, terrified of the graves, the ghosts, and the deathly atmosphere... and called for Mum and Dad.

Dad, a very light sleeper, was usually the one to get up in the night, but Mum came on the occasion I remember. She prayed for me and told me to pray to Jesus to take the dream away. 'Would Jesus stop the bad dreams?' I asked.

'Yes, he would,' she assured. For the next period of perhaps several years, whenever I prayed before going to bed, I did not have bad dreams, but when I forgot to pray, that dream recurred or I had a similar one. To this day, I usually remember to pray for good dreams and deliverance from bad ones—especially if I'm in a hotel room or unfamiliar place. This simple lesson gave me an underlying confidence that God answers prayer, that he loves and cares for us... and that the spiritual world is big, sometimes scary, and never very far away.

The second memory of answered prayer came when I was about eleven or twelve years old. We lived at that time farther north in Canada on a remote and rustic farmstead surrounded by forest. About a quarter mile from the timber-frame house stood a log barn, and just beyond the barn, our only water supply: a well with an old-fashioned hand pump. One of the regular chores shared between us boys and Dad (who probably did most) was to pump water by hand and carry it to the house in a bucket. Besides the arm-ache of that, the pump had to be primed with about a half gallon of water (boiling hot in the winter). Without priming, the old pump creaked and groaned, but stayed bone dry.

One very cold winter day, it was my turn to get the water and I trudged out to the well. Just as I hung my empty bucket on the spout, I realised I hadn't brought water to prime the pump. I was desperate enough to pray. I just couldn't bear the thought of walking back, heating a kettle, and returning again in the bitter cold and deep snow.

'Lord, could you please, just this one time, make the pump work without being primed?'

I tried the handle. To my surprise, water came immediately. 'Thank you, Jesus!'

It was a great lesson in the kindness of God; the gospel 'pump' has been primed by Jesus—be assured, no man has it in himself even to repent apart from the kindness of God. *'But God shows his love for us in that while we were yet sinners Christ died for us.'* (Romans 5:8) and *'Do you not know that God's kindness is meant to lead you to repentance?'* (Romans 2:4)

*Vance Royal Olson*

## Overcoming Fear

In my mid to late teens, I went through a period of drifting away from God and also came under an even more sinister attack of fear than the nightmares of my childhood. This time it was the fear of apparitions—of spirits or ghosts actually appearing in my presence. When I slept, I slept well with no disturbing dreams; but getting to sleep in the first place—or, worse still, waking up in the night—held a dread I could hardly bear. I hated to be alone at night. At one level it was a fear of darkness—sometimes it helped to leave the light on. Other times, the only thing that gave some relief was to drive around in my car. Remembering my childhood dreams, I would pray to God for help, recommit my life to him, and eventually get to sleep. But at morning light I forgot about God and returned to living as I pleased without reference to him.

As time passed, the problem grew more severe. Each time I prayed and then forgot about it next morning made it more difficult to believe God would help the next time. Sometimes I was fine for weeks, but then the fear would randomly return with a vengeance. At its worst, darkness surrounded me as if to close in on my mind, at which point I thought spirits, ghosts, demons or the devil would become visible to my physical eyes. Sometimes the little circle of light grew perilously small, despite my best efforts. One night I cried out in desperation to God, 'Lord I can't even repent because I just drift away from you again when the fear is gone—even though you have rescued me many times.'

After that I had some relief, but the fear never went away completely. Things got better when I finished school and went to live with my brother in a city several hundred miles away. I recommitted my life to the Lord and, with the fellowship of my brother and his Bible-school friends, was able to keep going forward in my faith. Perhaps the fear was behind me for good. Then my brother went away for a couple of weeks and I was alone in the apartment. Fear, worse than ever, gripped me as soon as night fell. I got up, switched on the lights, paced around for a while then went out for a drive in the car. Obviously this was unsustainable—I had work early next morning.

I begged the Lord for help and this time, unlike previous times, a clear thought began to develop in my mind: 'This fear is sin.' First reactions to that might be a sarcastic, 'Great, guilt on top of fear!' But when God speaks, even if at first it seems unreasonable or severe, the end result is always freedom, never guilt.

A few days later I went out to a summer Bible camp that some of my brother's friends were attending. The preacher was talking about getting free from sins and he had a wooden cross—roughly constructed from a couple of tree branches—standing at the front. Near the cross was a table with small pieces of paper and pins on it. We were invited to come up, take a paper, and write on it the sin we wanted to be free from. I went forward, got my paper, returned to my seat and wrote 'fear'. When everyone had done this we were called to come forward again and pin that 'sin' on the cross. To conclude the meeting, the cross with all its papers would be taken down to the lakeshore and burned. Several appeals were made but I stayed in my seat. It all seemed a bit intense and I rationalised that burning a cross couldn't be a good thing... perhaps it was weird and cultish? So I stuffed the paper in my jacket pocket and went home.

Several nights later, still alone in the apartment, fear gripped me again. I got out of bed, switched on the lights, got dressed, and was about to go out for a drive in my car. When I reached into my jacket pocket for the key, there was the paper with 'fear' written on it. 'Hmm... I'll burn it now.' I struck a match over the kitchen sink and it was ash in a few seconds. Instantly the fear left me.

I went back to bed and had a vivid dream that consisted of a series of close-up scenes from a large city. There were no iconic landmarks in view to identify the city, but I assumed it was San Francisco because some of the images were of sexual perversion, occultism and witchcraft. (I had recently seen a film series called *How Should We Then Live* by Francis Schaeffer in which a glimpse of such images had been associated with San Francisco.) As I was considering that the city must be San Francisco—still within the dream and seeing the images—the voice of God spoke clearly over it all: 'You will be at war with Satan in this city.' Then I woke up.

Only a few years later, I stood on an ordinary street in London, identical to one of the scenes from the dream.

However, the words God spoke in the dream refer to more than London; rather, *'...the great city which is spiritually called Sodom and Egypt, where their Lord was crucified.'* (Revelation 11:8) This is Babylon, Tyre, Nineveh, Jericho and even the 'Jerusalem' of Jesus' crucifixion. It is the city of men in rebellion against God. It is the world. It is the serpentine matrix of loveless power and false love. It is the kingdom of darkness on earth.

## Pressure

After getting free from fear, my life greatly improved, but of course it wasn't all sweetness and light. I was soon experiencing pressure—bombardment of my mind and heaviness of heart—that some days seemed almost unbearable. I remember my slight chagrin when, on several occasions, my brother broke into a rendition of, 'God has not promised skies always blue, flower-strewn pathways all our lives through ...' in response to the obvious heaviness of my heart. (No doubt I had some self-pity going on too!)

I didn't find out until years later that the New Testament word translated into English with words like: 'affliction', 'trouble' and 'tribulation', is the Greek word 'thlipsis' which literally means 'pressure'. For example, the word is used by Jesus when he said, *'In this world you will have 'pressure'; but be of good cheer, I have overcome the world.'* (John 16:33—usually translated 'tribulation') 'Tribulation' seems to carry the connotation of exotic religious 'end-times' happenings, so we miss the comfort of Jesus' words. Truly, he is speaking of the resistance we all feel in walking with him against the grain of this world in our day-to-day lives.

During this time of pressure, I had two memorable dreams. The first was a simple glimpse of Jesus walking ahead of me on a dangerous jungle path. Tribal warriors were hiding in the undergrowth and shooting at us with arrows, darts and spears. I was afraid and wanted to draw back but at the same time recognised that the only safe place was right up near Jesus. More than just information about the battle, this dream carried grace that helped me stay closer to Jesus; it carried the drawing love and desire of the Holy Spirit. Spiritual pressure tends to isolate us and cause us to think smaller, whereas the Holy Spirit brings us into spacious places and freedom.

Helpful though this dream was, the relentless pressure continued—especially against my mind. I soon began to resent the pressure and my thoughts started to run along the lines: 'Why don't God and the devil take their fight somewhere else away from me? I hate this pressure!' I began to imagine some such place; a rest, away and outside of the pressure; a cool, spacious, free, outside place... *outer rest*. The term 'outer rest' began to play on my mind. I was strongly and increasingly drawn toward this 'outer rest' and the protests of my conscience grew weaker and weaker. Then I had a second dream.

In the dream, a friend was giving me a guided tour through a cave that had been fitted out as a museum of the occult. The labyrinth of dark underground passageways had display modules, each with a glass front built into the walls. As we came to display after display, I turned my head away and refused to look in—I knew the images were hideous and loathsome horrors. Then we came to a particular exhibit and my friend, half humorously and half mockingly, pretended to be a tempter. 'Come to the outer rest!' he repeated several times while directing my gaze toward the display with dramatic gestures. I looked and saw a little label: 'The Outer Rest', with only darkness behind it. Then the voice of God boomed across the dream: 'THERE IS NO REST FOR THE WICKED.' I sat bolt upright in bed, wide awake. Whether that was the 'audible' voice of God or not, I don't know, but it was certainly very loud in the dream and it shook my whole being to the core.

I conclude that the 'outer rest' is one of the devil's wishful fantasies. Indeed it may be quite central to his kingdom of deception. It is the place he imagines as his own, where God is subject to his judgements and dictates. It is the outside place of overview that the serpent taught Eve to imagine; the 'refuge of lies' and 'shelter of falsehood' from Isaiah (28:15); and the 'high mountain' of Jesus' wilderness temptation. While purported to be outside, objective and neutral, the 'outer rest' is in truth no more than a shadow surrounded by the all-consuming fires of heaven; a diminishing island of insane folly; the proverbial, never possessed, 'hope in hell'.

Just as walls of darkness seemed to be closing in on me when I battled fear, the walls of heaven's fiery light close in on the serpent's darkness. And just as I feared seeing apparitions or spirits, the serpent fears what he will see when the walls of fire finally close in on his bastion of lies. For then he will see the beautiful Son of God himself; and in him, the glory to which every son was destined... and then... with Christ, the many sons conformed to his image. (Ref: Romans 8:19, 29) And in that seeing, the ancient serpent, ruler of this world and liar from the beginning, is judged by inexorable truth at last.

And here we might well pause to consider what manner of mind or spirit or being or person has come to such an unholy end, that the fires of all-consuming love—of beauty, truth and goodness uncloaked at last—should be to it the fires of destruction, of unmaking? That no part of it—though once conceived and birthed by beautiful love—any more contains anything with which love or beauty should find resonance or harmony? That passing love's filtering flame, no single vestige or trace remain! *'For there is no rest, says my God, for the wicked.'* (Isaiah 57:21)

The pressures we feel are the serpent's last desperate resistance to the inexorable day of his demise. If we could see it clearly—which of course we rarely do in the midst of it all—we would count it a great honour to be standing with Jesus, light of the world, as the final crush on darkness is levied.

## Training and Commissioning

For my training and commissioning, God chose to connect me with two ministries based in the UK and Europe. The first was Capernwray Bible School, a ministry of the Capernwray Hall Missionary Fellowship of Torchbearers, headed up at that time by its founder, Major Ian Thomas (British Army, WWII). From this ministry I learned faith of that particular kind that views every obstacle, interruption, coincidence or resistance as a step into something greater God will do. Major Thomas had built his organisation (Bible schools and other ministries in about 60 countries) by this faith and imparted it to his fellow workers. I remember, for example, his story of how a flat tyre on an Austrian mountain road had resulted in the boy who helped him receiving salvation in Jesus and some years later founding a Bible school in that same area. The irritation and trouble of one flat tyre had been turned into victory by God. That was the Major's faith in action and every student of his Bible schools seemed to catch at least a bit of it.

It became quite normal for me during that year to respond to difficulty by looking with eyes of faith for what God would do to turn it around for good. Life gets interesting in this dynamic of faith and, as I record in a later chapter, the cross of Jesus is ultimately the great turnaround for every bad thing that has ever happened. The reality of Jesus' death and resurrection energises the life of prayer and spiritual warfare through the conduit of faith.

I learned to apply faith to situations big and small throughout the year, and for a little 'cherry on top', on my final day, one of our singing teams (who were staying an extra week) stood on the railway platform and sang, 'Give me faith, enough to see me through, help me Lord to depend on you ...' as our train rolled out of Friedrichshafen station. The vivid clarity of word and song pierced the dull atmosphere of the station, puzzled the busy German commuters with air from another world, and fixed a moment of eternal joy in my heart.

The second ministry, Ichthus Christian Fellowship, founded by Roger and Faith Forster, was based in London, England. Roger had been one of the guest lecturers at the Bible school and I had, in the library near the end of the school year, discovered and devoured a copy of his *God's Strategy in Human History*. It was through this book, and more teaching the following year in London, that I began to put order and understanding around many of my experiences and lessons from the preceding years.

In the battles recounted in this book, credit for any victories attained must be given to the place of the whole Ichthus team and the corporate authority we carried together. No individual could accomplish the things I mention without a unified team and worshipping church standing in properly understood and applied biblical knowledge and truth. For that foundation I will be forever grateful for Roger's faithfulness to the Bible and especially his diligent and careful interpretation—even a slight question in his voice on a complex issue of interpretation could provide guidance at a confusing juncture in an impossibly complicated battle. He taught scripture in the anointing of the Holy Spirit and the accompanying power to establish God's will and kingdom on earth. This is an essential foundation for effective prayer, intercession and spiritual warfare.

My commissioning from God came after the first couple of months in London, at the beginning of the 'Network' course in church planting and inner-city evangelism. Somewhere in Belgium, on the road between London and southern Germany, God had spoken the words, 'Place your hands on my hydraulic system—where my Spirit is moving under pressure.' Here, we pick up my story at the beginning of the training course, in September 1983.

## CHAPTER 3
# THE LONDON SCENE: GATES OF THE CITY

Because the Bible often uses place locations in connection with meaning, I thought an introduction to the significant places I was involved with in London during my early years there would be helpful. Besides that, I can remember events at locations more easily than pinning down the exact date or sequence in some cases.

The main thrust of the prayer, intercession and spiritual warfare that I was being led into during this period related to the roots and consequences of World War II, and each of the locations incorporated this motif; each physical location or building and the people based there related to the war in various ways. How God sets up this kind of thing is hard to exactly put your finger on, but it's the kind of thing I really like. God is an 'omni-dimensional poet' whose words are time and space and material—of which the foundations were laid in the first three days of creation. To see God's ways in these dimensions is the essence of prophetic vision. I won't keep 'harping on' about it at every juncture, but keep an eye out for the wartime references as we go. I hope and pray you'll get a glimpse of the poem—and get caught up in many similar poems in your own life!

*Vance Royal Olson*

## ICHTHUS HOUSE

When I arrived back from my trip to Germany, I walked into the hallway of Ichthus House where I would be based for the training year. There on the narrow hall shelf were my motorcycle gloves—just as I had left them the week before. I picked them up and carried them and the rest of my luggage to the top floor where my room was. Thankfully I had been given a room of my own—a rare benefit of my infamous loud snoring! This little room, up in the roof peaks, was to be my study and bedroom for the coming academic year.

Ichthus House, an Edwardian mansion, had been purchased by ICF (Ichthus Christian Fellowship) from its former owner; an elderly spinster, Miss Spillman, who, as part of the deal, still lived in a flat at the back of the middle floor of the house. Originally owned by a London alderman, the house had come into the possession of Miss Spillman's father sometime before the war. Throughout my year there, I drank many cups of tea with Miss Spillman, now in her eighties, as she recounted the histories of house, family and area. She was prone to adding Bailey's Irish Cream liqueur to tea or coffee and so the conversation sometimes disintegrated into a dozy muddle before too long... but there was always tomorrow. Indeed it was difficult to pass her door—between my room and the meeting rooms downstairs—without being invited in for tea, perhaps on the pretext of a minor domestic chore. I guess she had been lonely in the years since her father and sister had died, and now couldn't believe her luck: a house full of students! (Who also met that need, which certain old ladies have, to moan and complain about someone... which in turn benefitted the students' characters—so it was highly satisfactory all round!)

The house had barely escaped destruction during the war. Bombs had landed front and back, blasting craters in the gardens and shattering windows; but the structure had survived—evidence of the superior skills of the legendary Edwardian builder, Ted Christmas—according to Miss Spillman! Mr Spillman's cork factory had not been so fortunate, nor had it been rebuilt after the war, the demand for corks having decreased with the advancement of other technologies.

In all Miss Spillman's ramblings about the era before the war, during the war, and after the war, I found pleasure to my soul. She noted all the little details and nuances of life that history books never do, but which old ladies excel at. Her father had been the first person in Upper Norwood to get a motor car: I sat with her (so to speak) on its leather seat while the neighbours looked on enviously. 'But that was in the twenties—a long time before the war.'

'We moved to this house later—a few years before the war—a London alderman had it built—the garden was lovely, with beautiful flower beds—they had parties in the garden, you know.' I huddled with her and her sister in the cellar while 'Jerry' did his worst to the prize-winning garden. 'I took care of the gardens—the flowers—

my sister liked to be indoors.' And I stood with her next morning: dismayed at the shattered remains of the fine Edwardian bay window.

And I was beside her when she opened the door to her crestfallen father on the day the factory went up in smoke. 'Still, we mustn't worry. It was never rebuilt, you know. But we got some money—after the war. That's how it was done. It was a cork factory—all manner of corks—all the bottles used corks then.'

The lectures for the course, daily worship and prayer times, the weekly leadership team meeting, as well as other church meetings all took place in two large reception rooms on the ground floor. The church office occupied a smaller room on the ground floor too, and behind the office, the kitchen and dining areas. On the two upstairs floors there were eight bedrooms besides Miss Spillman's flat. In the garden, immediately beyond the rear reception room's French doors, a baptistery had been dug and it was here that I was baptised again.

This baptism was a full immersion in water but for me it mainly concerned being baptised in the Holy Spirit. It was this that opened my imagination or spirit to a new level of prayer. Speaking words in prayer is a good thing but as the old saying goes: 'A picture is worth a thousand words.' To work directly in prayer by pictures in the mind or 'open visions' enables much more to be said and accomplished than words alone—words and pictures together is best of all.

The apostle Paul used various military images such as 'swords', 'armour' and 'strongholds'. These metaphors were no doubt active in his imagination as he also spoke out words in prayer. *'For though we live in this world we are not carrying on a worldly war, for the weapons of our warfare are not worldly (KJV 'Carnal') but have divine power to destroy strongholds. We destroy arguments and every proud obstacle to the knowledge of God, and take every thought captive to obey Christ...'* (2 Corinthians 10:5) In another place the apostle likens his spiritual warfare in Ephesus to 'fighting with beasts': *'What do I gain if, humanly speaking, I fought with beasts at Ephesus?'* (1 Corinthians 15:32)

The imagination that is baptised in the Holy Spirit is able to 'picture' the battle with various images, which enables us to transpose many areas of knowledge and understanding into spiritual authority in prayer. One of my earliest experiences of this occurred when I had been asked by the leadership to pray into a conflict between builders doing some renovation work at Ichthus House. As I prayed into the situation, I saw a picture in my spirit of one man holding on to the other man's work and dragging it down or resisting it. I knew this was God's interpretation of the situation because I had not yet started working with them myself and didn't have any opinion about who was right or wrong. I had a memory as a child of putting out salt in the cellar of our house to keep the salamanders away—the salt stung their skin, and they fled from it like a deadly poison. In my imagination and with words, I released 'salt' against 'the man' that was hindering the work. Of course this was not really the man, but an unclean spirit that he was allowing by his competitive and controlling attitude. When the salt hit, the spirit writhed and winched like any old salamander would, and then let go and fell away from the project. The atmosphere and efficiency of the renovations greatly improved after that.

In a similar way I began to learn how to use skills I had gained in other areas—mechanical and engineering. The first time was with the first tool I had learned to use as a child: a screwdriver. I was praying with a few other people for a woman who was being oppressed by spiritualism, and I could perceive in the spirit a hardened black substance sticking to her. The words I was using didn't seem to be affecting it and the idea came to mind: I need a tool to break this stuff off her. A screwdriver was at hand (in the spirit) so I picked it up and began to use it to prise off the resistant substance. In this case I was mainly praying in tongues and labouring in my mind or imagination, breaking the resistance bit by bit. A very helpful aspect of this kind of prayer is that a person can see what is being done and therefore knows how long to keep going. The end result was that the woman came into freedom.

An even more significant use of this kind of connection, between the various realms of knowledge that we all have, concerns intimacy with God the Father. The reason I was able to make the connection I recounted in the prologue between my earthly father and my heavenly Father is because of this baptising of the mind by the Holy Spirit, which came partly through Bible teaching. Roger had—right there in Ichthus house—powerfully taught about the intimacy Jesus had with the Father, and how in the

Holy Spirit, we too can have that same intimacy. Take Jesus' prayer in Gethsemane, for example: *'Abba, Father, all things are possible to thee...'* (Mark 14:36) The word 'Abba' is a child's intimate word, equivalent to something like 'daddy' or 'dad' in English.

The Apostle Paul makes the connection for our own hearts: *'...but you have received the spirit of sonship. When we cry, "Abba! Father!"'* (Romans 8:15) *'And because you are sons, God has sent the Spirit of his Son into our hearts, crying, "Abba! Father!" So through God you are no longer a slave but a son, and if a son then an heir.'* (Galatians 4:6-7)

It is because of these words brought to life in the Holy Spirit that I was able to connect with God the Father in the same tender and intimate way that I had with my earthly father as a little child. God the Father entered that secret place of deep love... I could call him 'Dad'. Of course my imperfect love had to be redeemed and perfected by Jesus, through His Abba Father's perfect love, and brought to me again in the Holy Spirit. Jesus himself prayed for this to happen for us in the great climax of his high priestly prayer: *'I made known to them thy name, and I will make it known, that the love with which thou hast loved me may be in them, and I in them.'* (John 17:26) This connection with the Father is the absolute bedrock foundation of all intercession and spiritual warfare—indeed of all ministries and all life. For, truly, the light that proceeds and comes forth from his great heart is the light of the world.

*Vance Royal Olson*

## The Dietrich Bonhoeffer Memorial Church

A short walk from Ichthus house, the fellowship regularly rented, for larger meetings, a church building belonging to a German Lutheran congregation. Even during the war there had been a German population in London—under suspicion and hard pressed no doubt—but surviving all the same, even to the present day. Sometime in the 1930s, before war broke out, Dietrich Bonhoeffer had been pastor of this London congregation. He returned to Germany as war was beginning and, despite the dangers, worked with others in opposing the Nazis. He was eventually imprisoned and put to death by direct order of Adolf Hitler. After the war, the London congregation renamed their building to honour him.

During my first few years in London, this building was the place where beautiful worship and anointed teaching and preaching took place. Many significant spiritual revelations and breakthroughs were released here—some of which will come up in later chapters. One example helps introduce the martyrdom connection so I'll touch on it here.

One Sunday night during the worship, someone shared a picture of a teardrop falling from the eye of Jesus into our midst. She described in slow-motion detail how it fell, as if it were a beautiful and precious diamond that sparkled in every direction. As she went on to prophesy that we are healed by his tears, and others also joined in with similar affirming words, I received a beautiful touch of healing to my heart and soul. My personal journey relating to this is recorded later, but for now I want to consider a wider aspect.

People often wonder why Jesus wept, for example, at the tomb of Lazarus. Why cry if you know he is going to be raised from the dead in a few minutes anyway? Similarly, why weep over martyrs if their deaths are actually going to bring good? And yet we cannot help but feel sorrow when we think of someone like Dietrich Bonhoeffer who was so cruelly killed only a few months before the war ended. Does Jesus, who wept at Lazarus' tomb and over Jerusalem, also weep over Dietrich Bonhoeffer and over London? I would say yes, and furthermore, that those tears are cleansing and healing tears.

Likewise, God the Father wept over his Son at Calvary, and continued to weep over him when he received his spirit and held him in his arms in Hades. How could he possibly not have? And the tears that fell from the Father's eyes, like great splashing diamonds, during the hours in Hades also washed the sins of the whole world out of His son's soul, and raised Him back to life again. Similarly, the tears of Jesus had washed the sorrow and death out of the souls of Mary and Martha and Lazarus.

The great joy and privilege of intercessors is to join our tears with the tears of the Father, Son and Holy Spirit for the cleansing away of sin and death from whatever place he may choose to send us. For that, we must know the cross in our own hearts. Indeed, no intercessor is 'worth their salt' if they haven't spent some time at Calvary blending their tears with the Father's tears for his Son. Zechariah prophesied the heart of this when he wrote: *'... when they look on Him whom they have pierced, they shall mourn for Him, as one mourns for an only child, and weep bitterly over Him, as one weeps over a first born.'* (Zechariah 12:10)

Another thing that happened for me at the Bonhoeffer Memorial Church was that one night in a meeting, a lady—I think it may have been the same lady who saw the teardrop—prophesied that someone was called to intercession for the nations. Strangely, the vision was of a copper teapot... I can't remember how she made the connection... but I had felt led by the Holy Spirit only a few hours earlier to fast from tea and coffee to focus prayer into the stronghold of Mormonism in connection with the war-dead of World War II. Other prophesies followed to confirm this word and prayers were made for the release of grace and wisdom in spiritual warfare for the nations. I remember Roger Forster praying specifically for me for knowledge and wisdom when I responded to this word. His tone—as it seemed to me at the time—implied that I didn't know much yet, which offended me slightly. I was already imagining that I knew quite a bit—I had only recently had the miraculous trip across Germany and other miraculous answers, after all! Pride, you see, is always the ever-present danger with knowledge of every kind. Oh, Lord, please deliver us from pride, every moment of every day!

This commissioning into intercession within the church corresponded to my earlier calling from God on the road in Belgium: first a call from God, then confirmation in the church, along with ongoing fellowship and teaching. We are members of God's family and household and will never reach our potential outside it.

## THE NEW LIFE CENTRE

In East Greenwich, which was my 'patch' for the training year, we (ICF) were working with a small independent church (formerly East Greenwich Baptist, renamed 'New Life'), having been invited to help by the elderly pastor. This pastor had been a successful professional photographer working for *Picture Post* magazine (iconic British photo journal 1938-1957) and became a Christian through his assignment covering the Billy Graham Haringay Crusade in 1954. (The thing that had impressed him most was that when he was taken into the team prayer meeting after Billy Graham had preached, everyone, including Billy himself, fell on their faces before God and prayed, 'Lord, keep him humble!'.)

The pastor's wife, a German woman who had married him before the war, became a Christian herself a few years after he had; though even now, in her seventies, she didn't seem entirely at peace with being a poor pastor's wife—having chosen, in the first place, a dashing celebrity photographer. Besides that, she still carried the wounds of living through the war as a German in London. But she did her very best with it all—a kind of complicated mix of hopelessness and kindness. For my part, I laboured to connect with the kindness.

The rest of the congregation consisted of three elderly ladies, a couple of students, an army musician in his mid twenties, and one or two occasional visitors. One of the ladies was a retired and recently widowed missionary. She had also lived through the war in London, and had lost a brother on the fighting front. In their grief and despair, her family had turned to spiritualism, that had in truth—despite the usual claims of contacting the departed—aggravated and extended the misery throughout all the family relationships for several generations (as spiritualism usually does if not put in check by prayer). She had become a Christian a few years after the war, married an older Pakistani man (a frightful scandal at the time on both counts), and spent thirty years or so in Pakistan as a missionary—or at least as the wife of a church planter. When I arrived, she was as complicated as the pastor's wife, but twice as forceful. Some days she was my staunchest ally; the next, my harshest critic. In the end I won her over—more because of my naiveté to her complex machinations than because of any wisdom I possessed—and she became a loyal prayer warrior. God is wise though. Who else would send a farm boy from the western prairies of Canada into such a matrix?

The building itself was a reworked and extended version of the old Sunday school hall—the main church building had been demolished and replaced by retirement flats. This building became one of my main places of prayer and a 'cameo' or 'stage' for many wider battles. The elderly pastor, who had overseen the building and decorating work, guarded it like his most precious possession and wouldn't suffer a single stain or cookie crumb on its virgin carpet—even a serious evangelistic or pastoral conversation had to give way to his fastidious brush and dustpan!

I perceived the building to be a stumbling block, and one of my first prophetic actions—under cover of a children's club—was to turn the entire main hall into the deck of a sailing ship, complete with mast and sail that reached the roof, and a painted sunrise mural to replace the velvet curtains at the front. God prefers sailing ships, especially those blown by the wind of His Spirit. About eight months after this, I stood one day on a beach in Normandy, France, when God asked me, 'What shall we do with the sea?' Before thinking, a cry came from my heart by the Holy Spirit: 'Oh, let's just have sailing ships!' I didn't connect it with this 'sailing ship prayer' at the time, but with hindsight I understand it as God's answer and affirmation. After all, prophetic action is 'acted out' prayer which God answers.

And then there was the history of the building and the congregation to deal with. The connection between spiritual conditions in the present and events of the past covers a range from obvious physical or financial elements to the more subjective emotional or spiritual perceptions. Sensing of 'atmospheres' corresponding to historical events in a particular place is common to many people, especially those with an artistic or literary disposition—whether Christian or not. This sensing of atmosphere is of course just another way of talking about discernment and, as we'll discuss later, is a combination of knowledge (deduction of universals) and desire (feeling of attraction or repulsion) along with revelation (vision, picture, word, impression, etc.).

Like all the thriving pre-war churches, East Greenwich Baptist had diminished during and after the war, both from a direct loss of young men and from the loss of heart by many Christians—almost every London family had suffered death, long-term separation, and financial loss. In the 1970s, the struggling remnant of the East Greenwich congregation was further savaged by an ultra Calvinistic pastor, who added early charismatic 'wackiness' to the mix. He convinced half the congregation to move to Scotland with him on the basis of a doubtful prophetic word that the Southeast of England was going to be swept away in a flood. Most of the remaining traumatised members had scattered, but in the cellar we found damp and musty old record books with names and addresses. After a lot of prayer with colleagues, I felt we should visit as many of these people as we could. When this was done, we sensed a door had been closed and old grievances put to rest.

Just after that, however, I became aware in my heart of a pastor from a much earlier period. I could see him in an open vision, sitting at his desk in a black Victorian suit with a very defiant demeanour. I'm not necessarily saying

I was seeing the man himself; it could have been a spiritual stronghold revealed as a person by the Holy Spirit. Nevertheless it was clear that a particular pastor was responsible for the stronghold being present, and the vision was a working view of my battle with that spiritual stronghold.

In the passages in Romans where the apostle Paul seems to be addressing a particular person (sometimes called the 'straw man'), I believe he may have been experiencing something similar to this: seeing a 'spiritual stronghold' or 'theological error' personified in a vision. (This is one example of how 'knowledge' and 'spirit' interface.)

I engaged in prayer by 'preaching' at this man in my vision. Sometimes I did this out loud as I prayed in the building (not of course in meetings) and at other times it was just in the back of my mind. Truth after truth, revelation after revelation I threw at this 'guy' but he never seemed to flinch; he had heard it all before—a 'religious spirit' for sure. For several weeks I even exposed him to the anointed preaching that I was regularly hearing from the ICF leadership team at the time, but even that didn't shift him. And then one day, in a seemingly quite bland moment, I said to him, 'It is possible to be perfect.' On hearing those words, he immediately bowed down in repentance, and disappeared from my sight. The vision closed.

The religious spirit effectively blames God for sin by convincing people that it is impossible to be perfect. If this doctrine was true, we would, by definition, not be responsible for our sin. But since sin, by definition, is that which we *are* responsible for, the doctrine that perfection is impossible is obviously self-contradictory and false. It may seem like a fine point, and I'm not saying that anyone other than Jesus has ever achieved perfection, but the moment we allow this teaching, we open a door to self-pity and blaming God for our sins rather than taking responsibility and finding grace and forgiveness. In front-line spiritual warfare and in the laying of solid foundations in church planting, this level of truth is not optional.

Every false teaching either is, or potentially is, a doctrine of demons: a doorway that gives demons access into our lives and churches. A group of people adhering to a false doctrine (sometimes just by fuzzy thinking) provides a dwelling place for an unclean spirit. The doctrine in this case is the 'set of knowledge-based details', or the 'set of universals' (more on 'universals' later) and desire is furnished in the first instance by people who choose the doctrine as an alternative to repenting of sin—which of course suits the sinful fallen angels very well indeed. Hence a group of people holding a false teaching is a comfortable dwelling place for an unclean spirit.

Conversely, every truth is a doorway potentially for angels and the Holy Spirit. A group of people adhering to true doctrine provides a dwelling place for the Holy Spirit: the Spirit of truth. The more deeply truth is received, and especially obeyed, the more room there is for the Holy Spirit to dwell in us, individually and collectively, and for every heavenly blessing to overflow around us.

The desire comes from the Holy Spirit (ref: Galatians 5:17) who also heals our hearts and purifies our own desires. Therefore we are motivated by his 'love poured into our hearts' (ref: Romans 5:5), not by fear, determination or pride—which all lead to religious entanglements.

Before moving on, I should note that the perfection I'm speaking of here is sinlessness, not perfection in every area of life. Whose house could, or even *should*, ever be perfectly clean? Could any task be done perfectly? If I strove to make this book perfect even to my own standard (which would itself be far from perfect), it would never be finished in a lifetime. No; I'm simply speaking about sin—our choices. I'm not talking about mistakes, lack of skill or knowledge, or even weakness. The pursuit of perfection in a general sense is more likely to lead to a breakdown because it is an unbearable burden driven by pride and fear. The perfection I'm talking about is only available by the grace found in the Holy Spirit from Jesus, and its hallmark is humility and rest.

Of course there were many other battles to cleanse the building and the territory around it, which we will look at later, but to complete the picture, a day came when the battle over the building was finished. I was praying in the main meeting hall and declaring the cleansing power of the blood of Jesus, and the extreme power of holiness or 'separation' that occurred when Jesus rose from the dead—with clean hands and a pure heart, leaving sin in the grave. (Ref: Psalm 24:4; Romans 1:4) Deep in the Lord's presence, I perceived the power of the Holy Spirit cleansing the ground; first, down to the core of the Earth, and then, up into space to the very edge of the universe. The building was sanctified and the territory set aside for God's purposes. In the end, the entire Earth will be likewise cleansed, with no echo or lingering memory of evil to mar the brightness of its dawn.

## NUMBER 7 COMBEDALE ROAD

Besides the New Life Centre, the army musician in the congregation had a house around the corner that we used for an evening enquirers group, and sometimes to provide lodging for visiting student teams. During the first year, I stayed there myself one week—sleeping on the floor along with one such team—because Ichthus House was fully occupied by other teams. (A Canadian cousin, Phil Loseth, happened to be passing through that week and joined the rest of us on the floor—sorry for the low level of hospitality Phil!) It was an intense and pressurising week, partly because of some very 'unsavoury' books stored in our room.

The books were in the horror genre and, though I didn't look beyond the covers, the cover pictures themselves were horrid enough—demonised horse faces, skulls and that kind of thing. Our host was out most days, but since he was a member of the congregation and a friend, I decided to have a word with him about the books. When the busy week was over and I had moved back to my permanent room at Ichthus House, the moment came to address the topic. My plan was to take the casual approach. I didn't want to be controlling or intense so I planned my words carefully... something like, 'You have some books in this house that might not be too good...'

But when I opened my mouth to speak, these words came out instead: 'YOU HAVE A VERY EVIL BOOK IN THIS HOUSE!'

So much for the casual approach! My friend and colleague first whitened with fear and started trembling, but then went to a hidden shelf inside an unused chimney breast and brought out a classic ancient book of magic and witchcraft (I will not even write its title here).

We first prayed prayers of repentance and renouncing and then got rid of the book itself. In the sweetness of his penitent heart, my friend would not even allow me to touch any part of the book, so I prayed in the Spirit while he tore it page by page and burned it in the fireplace. When this was done, the whole house had a much more wholesome air, and the other books disappeared over the following days without me having to mention them. And my friend, who had previously had a series of failed and heartbreaking relationships, met and married a lovely girl before the year had passed. (More on their wedding later.)

One other thing happened at this house that is quite interesting. One day, three of us were praying there, against a religious spirit that was troubling a mutual friend in another church. Having gained access in the

Holy Spirit, I felt led to pray as I never had before—or since: I found myself commanding the religious spirit to bow down to Jesus. The anointing was so heavy that the spirit was forced to comply—but it sure wasn't happy about it. We finished our prayer time with thanks and praise and I left the house.

As I was walking down Combedale Road, the religious spirit appeared in front of me—visible... it seemed... to my physical eyes. It was in such a frenzy of rage and frustration that it couldn't even speak. I, by contrast, was surrounded by supernatural calm, and simply said, 'I don't have to listen to you.' At the same time as saying this—in the Spirit, without thinking why—I deliberately closed and opened my eyes in a slow blink. The evil spirit vanished and the scripture came to me: *'A king who sits on the throne of judgement winnows all evil with his eyes.'* (Proverbs 20:8) Then the Lord said, 'You've closed the door on that one forever.'

Apparently some demons are permanently put out of commission: perhaps *'...kept by Him in eternal chains in the nether gloom...'* (Jude 1:6) Incidentally, I have no dogmatic position to defend on this point—the story is told, as it seemed to me at the time, not as doctrine.

## THE HAUNTED HOUSE ON BEACONSFIELD ROAD

My second year working in East Greenwich, after finishing the training course, was as a full-time worker on a kind of 'internship'. I could no longer live at Ichthus House as it would be needed for the new intake of students in training. Little did I know, my training was about to continue in earnest—does one ever really graduate in the Kingdom of God?

The elderly pastor and his German wife occupied a small flat in a large house near the Church building and had free rent in exchange for managing the other flats and bedsits in the house, six or seven in all. They offered me a place in the house, which the congregation would pay for. It seemed the perfect solution.

A strange coincidence then occurred. Another Canadian, a young woman, had applied for one of the other vacant rooms in the house at the same time as I had agreed to move in. She moved in directly across the hall from my room about a week before me. So we each had a ground floor room at the front of the house; symmetrical rooms, same size, and each with a large bay window facing the street. Hmm...? Oh, and she had mental problems... very severe... social services and the police had been involved. The elderly pastor had been delighted to welcome two Canadians because of course everyone likes Canadians—what's not to like, right?—or perhaps rather, 'Eh?'

Unfortunately the old pastor's delight had long evaporated by the time I arrived a week later. My fellow countrywoman had seriously tarnished the image: gone the clean mountain air; gone the pristine mounted police with their triumphant scarlet coats; gone the maple leaf unfurled in the clean fresh breeze. Come instead:

drunken belligerence; hour-long tirades against people on TV—yes, she literally sat swearing at the TV for hours and hours on end. The whole house was in turmoil, the old pastor confounded.

The house itself was ancient—never redecorated, painted or modernised since long before the war—early twenties maybe—even World War I perhaps. The shared bathroom down the hall had an ancient brass gas boiler that had to be lit with a match to get hot water directly into the claw-foot cast-iron bath. It felt positively Victorian, as if I had stepped back in time by a hundred years or so—an aspect I quite liked.

But then, even apart from the new 'haunting' by the Canadian woman, I began to discern that the whole place was rather spooky. Sometimes the old pastor's wife shuffled down the hall and appeared at my door in the dim light bearing gifts—dented tins of soup she had acquired cheaply. Her face was so old and wrinkled, so laden with the wounds of the years, and her eyes were so probing of my responses that I had to muster all the good manners my mother had taught me just to remain civil. This house was heavy.

My compatriot was so loud at night that I had to play music to get to sleep. I got the longest-playing worship tape I could find, to drown out the sound and feeling of her constant shouting and cursing. In this way I held the night-time in a kind of equilibrium and was able to function somewhat normally… until I could develop a longer-term strategy, get some prayer going, and have some praying friends over for a good clear-out session.

## The Gates of Eden

One day in broad daylight—before I had time to organise any prayer—and when my Canadian tormentor had finally passed out or fallen asleep, I walked into my room to see two men relaxing in armchairs and talking in front of my fireplace. They appeared to be well-dressed golfers, and I estimated the time period: circa 1920. They looked up at me as I entered and our eyes met. I had not yet experienced any positive, Holy Spirit time breaches, and my first response was confusion and fear as my mind raced to comprehend the scene. They were obviously in a different time... Had I stepped into their time? Or had they entered mine? The feeling was dark and demonic. I froze momentarily. And then instinctively began speaking out in tongues—a very handy gift, in a tight spot. Instantly, the intruders vanished.

As I've come to understand it over later years, this was not actually a time breach at all—just demonic deception. Genuine time breaches, thankfully, are only available in the high heavens by the Holy Spirit and the holy angels. The devil can do no more than stage counterfeits; indeed, I believe it is of this high heavenly realm that Christ spoke when he said, *'I saw Satan fall like lightening from heaven.'* (Luke 10:18) Hence, Satan has not—since that instantaneous 'lightening' fall—had any ability to access exceptional connections in time. He must move from linear hour to linear hour, crawling in the dust of the earth, like the men he caused to stumble. His wings are clipped; his legs are gone: his ghosts are fakes. However, he did have some demons in my house. And they were obviously organised into a little stronghold!

It was time to take action. My first leading from the Holy Spirit came through teaching from Faith Forster (wife of Roger, and a leader and minister in ICF in her own right). She made the point—which I have never forgotten because it always cuts through a lot of super-spiritual nonsense—that if you can't take authority over your own bedroom in the natural realm, don't imagine that you can take authority over any demons in the spiritual realm. First action then was to thoroughly clean, tidy and take total dominion over my room, which was a large bedsit with a kitchenette in one corner, a table, a bed and a few chairs. I got it all shipshape. I even covered the extremely draughty front bay window with clear polythene, to give the small electric heater some hope of keeping the room warm. In short, I took authority over my room in every way I could.

I had barely finished, and was about to sit back to reflect, when an unholy commotion commenced across the hall. The mad Canadian woman had chosen this exact moment to totally destroy her room. Everything was in motion. The furniture was being smashed, plants and soil dumped on the carpets, dishes shattered, and a wooden chair sent clean through the large front bay window. She had done the exact opposite to me in her parallel and symmetrical room. It was in this occurrence that I first began to get an inkling of the 'dialectic' (argument or conflict) that the church engages in, on the 'stage' of this earth. Every thought we think and every action we take in the Holy Spirit imposes a pattern against the grain, or asserts a contrary will to what the enemy desires to do. (I will take up this understanding of dialectic in more detail in a later chapter.)

My next strategy was to bring in some prayer support. I had excellent and anointed friends, so I arranged a prayer meeting at my place one Saturday morning. We assembled and began to pray—and not whimpering petitions, either—real strong fighting prayer. The spiritual temperature rose. Shrieks were heard in the hall. We rushed out. The Canadian woman had the old pastor by the neck and seemed intent on strangling him. We intervened... a little brawn isn't always a bad thing in spiritual warfare. The old German wife called 999, and help arrived in minutes... the police can be good in a tight spot too. They took the woman away... and she was never seen by us again. We then continued with our prayer meeting, and from that day my house became, if not wonderful, at least a reasonable place to live.

One other thing happened in this house, which though not seemingly directly linked to the house, resides in my memory as a scene in the middle of my room there. I had been feeling very heavyhearted—even grieved, I would say—and had asked a couple of people to pray for me. These were not my old friends, but visitors from another church, who brought wisdom and grace from another spiritual stream. I sat in a chair in the middle of the room while they stood around me praying and prophesying. The word I remember is that the pain I was feeling in my heart was not because of something wrong, but because I was carrying the 'burden of the Lord'.

From this word, I began to understand that much effective prayer is too deep for words, but involves being in the world and in God's presence at the same time. 'Caring in the presence of God', I began to call it. Worldly wisdom would have us breezing through life in a bored and disengaged apathy to the sorrows all around us—'passing the wounded man on the other side of the road', so to speak. Our call, rather, is to share the redeeming sorrow of God the Father's great heart in the travail against evil. True spiritual warfare is never so simple as being the one in power, and pushing demons around. Don't rejoice that the demons are subject to you, Jesus once said, but rather that your names are written in heaven, engraved on the Father's hands and heart, and inscribed on a place at His table. (Ref: Luke 10:20; Isaiah 49:6)

# CHAPTER 4
# God's Hydraulics and the Right of Access: Gates of the Earth

*'Thus says the Lord of hosts: If you will walk in my ways and keep my charge, then you shall rule my house and have charge of my courts, and I will give you the <u>right of access</u> among those standing here.'*
(Zechariah 3:7)

In the months following my experience of seeing the Father's face, when I had cold hands while riding my CX500 Honda through Belgium, the Lord began to teach me about 'the right of access'. My earthly father had told me to hold on to the warm hydraulic oil pipes and control valve by which the tractor operator controlled the machine being pulled. My heavenly Father began to show me how his hydraulic system brought the power of heaven into operation on earth. Just as the power came from the tractor engine through the pump, control valve and hoses to the machine, the power of his great heart, perceived through his face, flowed into my heart and from there out to wherever he directed it should flow. *'The king's heart is a stream of water in the hand of the Lord; he directs it wherever he will.'* (Proverbs 21:1)

We have access to the Father, Paul tells us in the second chapter of Ephesians, and it was the experiential reality of this access which I was now being trained in. The promise to Joshua the priest in Zechariah 3:7 was: *'I will give you the right of access among those standing here.'* With access to the Father comes authority, but for him to direct it through our lives, we need access on earth as well. Access on earth comes through knowledge which is the interface between our mind and all the realities that knowledge corresponds to—those 'realities' include, of course, other minds. Knowledge is the 'language' of minds, we might say.

## DISCERNMENT AND THE KEY OF KNOWLEDGE

*'And it is my prayer that your love may abound more and more with knowledge and all discernment...'*
(Philippians 1:9)

*'Woe to you lawyers! for you have taken away the key of knowledge; you did not enter yourselves, and you hinder those who were entering.'*
(Luke 11:52)

*'Yet among the mature we do impart wisdom, although it is not a wisdom of this age or of the rulers of this age, who are doomed to pass away. But we impart a secret and hid-*

*den wisdom of God, which God decreed before the ages for our glorification. None of the rulers of this age understood this; for if they had, they would not have crucified the Lord of Glory.'*
(I Corinthians 2:6-8)

*'For though we live in the world we are not carrying on a worldly war, for the weapons of our warfare are not worldly but have divine power to destroy strongholds. We destroy arguments and every proud obstacle to the knowledge of God, and take every thought captive to obey Christ, being ready to punish every disobedience, when your obedience is complete.'*
(II Corinthians 10:3-6)

There are two systems of knowledge that operate on planet earth. We normally call the most obvious one 'the system'—often with a note of dismay or disapproval if it happens to be contrary to our wishes. We mean of course the whole system of economic, political and social powers; the conglomerate authority around us; how 'things work' in general. The Bible calls it the 'rulers of this age', 'the kingdom of this world' or sometimes just 'the world'.

This 'world' was the system of knowledge bought into by Adam and Eve. Ostensibly, man is at the top and in control of it. God, by contrast, has his own little box within it—the proprietor of the religious element of 'the system', one might say. In this religious part of the system, men analyse and judge their god by a sub-system they call theology. The process was started by the serpent back in Eden when he took Eve into his 'classroom' and sketched out one of his own little quandaries about God. (Sometimes the serpent calls his 'classroom' the 'outer rest' as we discussed earlier.)

Much theology since has consisted of debates around the serpent's quandaries, all of which can be boiled down to the confused analysis of love from the point of view of one who has already rejected love. These debates are always about the relative responsibilities between lovers and the supposed 'underlying' motivations of lovers. In the main they are: law and grace; faith and works; free will and determinism; and the various conservative and liberal issues. Within the serpent's classroom, these debates all carry a whiff of self-justifying frustration, bitterness and anger.

And of course none of these 'theological debates' is of any help to truehearted lovers at all. In fact they are all about as useful to true lovers as an ex-boyfriend or girlfriend would be as a live-in house guest and adviser to a newly married couple. (And that does seem to be approximately the scene when Eve and the serpent had their infamous chat.) All these 'theologies'—the great debates of the ages—arise from offenses with love and the serpent's 'classroom' itself is the domain of anger and offense. That 'classroom'—the 'serpent's head'—must be crushed beneath the 'heel' of Jesus, in each of us, if we are ever to think rightly. (Ref: Genesis 3:15)

The other system of knowledge was the one rejected

by Adam and Eve in Eden. It is the one where God is the head. It flows from his heart and mind with his thoughts and deeds; and man is a creature within it. It was lost to mankind with the first sin, but has now been made available again in Jesus who has become, once more, *'the head over all things for the church.'* (Ephesians 1:22) In this system or 'kingdom', knowledge has a secondary role to love and obedience; man is not given the outside overview; he is not the remote and neutral judge of good and evil; nor is he the analyser of love. In this system, love does not answer to knowledge, but knowledge answers to love.

Love is obedience without full understanding of all the reasons. Indeed, the pursuit of those reasons is itself a rejection or denigration of love because true love actually desires obedience deeper and beyond reasons. (Ask anyone who's really in love.) A 'reason' in this context would be an ulterior motive deeper than love. Therefore, a 'reason' by definition would be a violation of true love: giving knowledge the higher place. Love itself must be the reason and foundation. Like the old song says: 'Love me for the reason, and let that reason be love.' Beyond words and knowledge, love is the inscrutable ground—God—'love himself'—upon which all foundations are built. To see the depths of his love is the one thing that opens our hearts to love in return. *'We love, because he first loved us.'* (I John 4:19) God's love is the reason; and as you see him, you quite simply choose to love and obey him, or you don't. Of course this is a process and journey of a lifetime, but it still consists of actual choices at specific moments along the way.

The gate out of Eden was the choice not to obey; it was the choice not to love God. Adam and Eve chose the knowledge of good and evil (the 'reasons' ostensibly deeper than love) and rejected true knowledge, which is love and obedience—i.e., the actual experiential knowledge of God. Jesus made the opposite choice to Adam and Eve in his wilderness temptation, reaffirmed it day by day in his life, and finally established and proved it in saying 'not my will but yours' as he prayed in Gethsemane and accepted the cross. Jesus laying down his life on the cross is the revelation and actual giving to mankind of the deepest, truest and greatest love ever. Hidden *within*—and never *outside*—this obeying love is the key of true knowledge, the one key that opens all the gates of Eden.

## ACCESS: USING THE KEY OF KNOWLEDGE

'[God the Father, of Christ] ...*when he raised him from the dead and made him sit at his right hand in the heavenly places, far above all rule and authority and power and dominion, and above every name that is named, not only in this age but also in that which is to come; and he has put all things under his feet and has made him head over all things for the church, which is his body, the fullness of him who fills all in all.*'
(Ephesians 1: 20-23)

*'[of the church]... that their hearts may be encouraged as they are knit together in love, to have all the riches of assured understanding and the knowledge of God's mystery, of Christ, in whom are hid all the treasures of wisdom and knowledge.'*
(Colossians 2: 2-3)


*'For the desires of the flesh are against the Spirit, and the desires of the Spirit are against the flesh...'*
(Galatians 5:17)


Spiritual access, or the opening of the gates of Eden, functions through this true and hidden knowledge which corresponds to Jesus' headship on one hand and desire which flows in the Holy Spirit on the other. Jesus is our Joshua (given *'the right of access'*, Zechariah 3:7) who is head over all knowledge and it is the Spirit in our hearts directing us through his desires—which are the Father's desires. Of course, within Him, all desire and knowledge are in perfect unity: True love.

On the knowledge side, doorways or access into the spiritual world are available by our perception of universal features or 'universals' which are recurring 'motifs' or 'elements of design'. From these related details we abstract meaning; we derive a general principle. We perceive, for example, that a Great Dane and a Toy Poodle are both dogs by their 'doggy' look and 'doggy' behaviour, and that unmistakable 'doggy' smell. 'Doggyness' is the 'universal' or, rather, 'set of universals'; the collection of details by which we perceive that the creature before us is in fact a dog, and not a cat or cow. The human mind does this kind of thing constantly and knowledge is the drawing together or interpretation of facts and the collating of those facts into various categories, theories and explanations. The general term for this process is 'deduction'.

A mystery novel or real-life crime case is solved using deduction. Details or 'clues' which at first seem unrelated are later found to be part of a cohesive explanation. The theories of science also evolve by deduction. Einstein abstracted or deduced, from seemingly contradictory experimental evidence, the theories of special and general relativity.

Of course there are false deductions. These could arise either by honest error or because of predisposition or prejudice. In a breathtaking leap of counterintuitive presumption (a beautiful name for 'foolishness'—if I do say so myself), atheists exclude God from all their data—and yet have remarkable clarity about what this non-existing God must be like, in the event that he ever did decide to exist. Paranoid people deduce various conspiracy theories from evidence that a healthy mind would dismiss. At an extreme level, some mental illness drives people to use deduction in a deceptive and distorted way—imagining sinister plots in the pattern of words in a newspaper, or that they are being pursued by foreign agents, for example.

In a happier way, children and the childlike use deduction to imagine shapes and faces in the clouds, voices in repetitive sounds, and many similar things. Besides this wholesome (but not strictly true) imaginative element, it is always worth bearing in mind that all people (even the sanest) make mistakes. There is nothing unusual or mystical about the principle itself—we all use it at various levels every day. Because it is so common and normal, however, we often take it for granted and never develop it.

While I was beginning to understand all this, in the sort of philosophical way I have been speaking, my colleague Nigel, who was leading a church plant in another area, happened to tell me about a game he had been playing with some of the people in his congregation. I've heard of many people playing it since and you have probably heard of it or played it too. It goes like this: If so-and-so was a car, what car would they be? Or if such-and-such was a dog, what dog would it be? And so on. This kind of deduction or abstraction of universal or shared features is the kind of thing we all do from infancy.

One of the anecdotes from my childhood, which my mother told every time a zebra was in view or mentioned, involves the same process. My sister Marlys was under two years old and just learning to talk when we went to the zoo one day. As we stood by the fence looking at a zebra, she said in her cute baby talk: 'Dat tupos tu be a hoss.' This statement contains truths about which lengthy philosophical and scientific essays could be—indeed, *have* been—written, without adding much to its simple profundity. (In the first Appendix, I'll add some more!)

I often meditated on that profundity, during this period of learning to collate my experiences into a cohesive understanding. The other thing was the actual application of this in spiritual warfare and exerting the authority of heaven onto the earth: 'hydraulics'. And of course the use of this picture or metaphor (hydraulics) is itself an example of the same thing. The reason we often overlook this idea is that it is so intrinsically linked with ordinary language and everyday ways of understanding simple things. When the Holy Spirit begins to teach us, of course everything is taken to a different level and we could apply the biblical term, 'discernment', which begins in simple deduction, but adds experience or the 'time dimension' as well as supernatural revelation. I first heard the word 'discernment' mentioned by a visiting preacher, when I was about eleven years old. I thought it sounded like a beautiful word, so I asked God for it, just as the preacher said we should. I didn't even know what the word meant, of course... but God has been teaching me since that day.

One lesson in this whole area of knowledge and discernment as regards spiritual warfare occurred when I went with a colleague to a youth centre in Peckham—a fairly rough area in SE London. The room was smoky (various kinds) and crowded with local youths in a volatile mix of boredom and frustration. I had been taught that the key to successful evangelism is breaking spiritual strongholds through prayer and was beginning to grasp that the 'knowledge' or 'set of details' from which we abstract universal features is simply a house or dwelling place for spiritual beings. When I asked God for access to the spiritual realities of the situation 'or stronghold' to pray against, I found myself also searching in my heart for something like temptation—some kind of desire. In this particular case there seemed to be a coating of clear plastic over everything so I wasn't able to actually connect or have any effect on the atmosphere. I understood how the process worked but I wasn't ready to take on the demons present in this situation and Father was wisely shielding me from them. However, it was one of my first lessons in this kind of discernment: how knowledge and desire operated together.

Any spiritual stronghold consists of these two elements: the set of knowledge-based universal features and some kind of desire. The 'universal' or set of knowledge-based details on its own is an 'empty house'; whereas 'desire' on its own is a 'being' or 'spirit' without a house. The world is full of many such 'houses', some unoccupied, some partially occupied and some packed full. Then, too, there are a lot of beings—housed, un-housed and wrongly housed—and a whole lot of comings and goings.

This is the realm in which angels and demons along with their human collaborators are at war. The church, ultimately a dwelling place or stronghold for God on the earth, is itself, in this age, a warzone of conflicting beings trying to live in it. By prayer, teaching and right order or 'righteousness', we labour in the Holy Spirit under the headship of Christ, to make the church hospitable to God and his angels and hostile to his enemies, the fallen angels or demons.

In the early months of ministry training in East Greenwich, I had many lessons and experiences in this area of access. The normal pattern became: new revelation of Jesus and the Father (access to heaven), followed by encounter with the enemy (access on earth), who was defeated by the truth I had just received. Sometimes when a particular stronghold gave way through prayer, objective tokens of this breakthrough came when people held by that stronghold came to faith and joined the congregation.

Many of the early additions to the congregation were signs and wonders showing God's heart for all the nations. Answers to prayer had come through revelation of God's love corresponding to needs and wounds in nations and cultures—including the indigenous London culture. Before the congregation had reached fifty people, there were already seventeen different nationalities—and I had never consciously aimed at that diversity; it simply followed from the Spirit's leading in prayer and warfare.

At other times, victory over strongholds didn't relate directly to people joining the church but to other positive changes in the city or nation. The following sections give some examples to illustrate the principles and scope.

## UNBELIEF

To a 'new world' tourist, London is mysterious, ancient, quaint and crusty; but to the church-planting evangelist it is—or at least was in 1983—an immovable stronghold, a paradigm of recalcitrant unbelief. The skill to ignore and be unaffected had been developed and refined over long centuries to the degree that it would have made Chorazin and Bethsaida (rebuked by Jesus for unbelief) look like revival centres. Sometimes this ability to be unaffected—the legendary 'stiff upper lip'—can seem like a pillar of strength, such as during 'The Blitz'; but it can also become a stumbling block of unbelief.

During the first months of church planting, the weight of this unbelief was increasing against me, until one day while praying, I found myself standing in a vision on Blackheath, a grassy common crossed by several roads that I used most days on my way from Forest Hill (where I lived) to East Greenwich (where the church plant was). On the heath, in the vision, everything was as normal with the perpetual traffic and people: the red buses, the black cabs, the cars and the lorries. Everything was constant and unchanging. As if to emphasise the immovability, my eye was drawn to a large black rock embedded in the ground, like an almost submerged tombstone. This 'motif' or 'universal' or 'stronghold' of death and unbelief appeared to have been there for centuries. 'Nothing changes here' it declared.

This day, however, as I stood watching in the vision, the stone began to heave up from beneath until it cracked completely in half. I knew immediately that this was the power of the resurrection of Jesus penetrating the resistant atmosphere of old London. The resurrection is God's mighty turnaround in the midst of all the earth;

the great pivot in the whole age of man; nothing can ever be the same again because the power of death and unbelief is eternally cast out in the ever-present moment of Jesus rising from the dead. The vision lasted no more than a few seconds but it deposited faith in my heart that was so dynamic and full of energy that it was like an engine driving me through the atmosphere of unbelief over the months that followed. This was an essential moment of heavenly access, and one of the keys to all that came after.

## SPIRITUALISM

Connected with death and unbelief, one of the main strongholds I came up against during the first year working in Greenwich was spiritualism. Considering that I had first felt the call to the Greenwich area because I had heard of a witch's coven there, I guess this is hardly surprising. The spiritualism battle arose out of general prayer walking in the area. We had prayed over a spiritualist event at a pub called The Mitre and, the following day while door-knocking, were invited into a house where three people who worked at The Mitre were having tea together. Two of them responded to the gospel and joined our enquirers group. Besides that, these pub workers all knew a guy named Brian whom I was already following up from a mission event on Blackheath. I will tell Brian's story and how this spiritualism strand developed in a later chapter.

*The Gates of Eden*

## SLAVERY

One day while praying, not long after my motorcycle trip in Belgium and Germany when I had the revelation of Father's love and care for every cold person, I was carried in a vision to a slave ship loaded with African slaves—somewhere on the Atlantic and several hundred years into the past. I stood below the deck where they were roped tightly to rough-hewn beams, writhing in agony as the ice-cold salt water splashed over their open wounds. My attention was drawn to four in particular, and as I felt Jesus' and the Father's heart of love flowing out toward them, the beams gave way, like a wooden gate opening. Then the vision closed as smoothly as it had opened. The following Sunday four black people joined the congregation—not as a group or even from the same country; 'just happened' to come on the same day.

## FASHION

It is not only in the church that spiritual warfare or the release of God's authority is relevant. He is the Lord of the whole earth and has an interest in every aspect of human life. One day during this period, while walking through a busy shopping area, I was vaguely thinking about fashion. My thought ran along the lines of, 'Why does the "in fashion" actually look more attractive, beautiful and sexy? And why does the "out of fashion" look have such a drab "un-coolness" about it?' I know that some religious folk put this down to lustful, evil fashion gurus trying to lead us down one titillating path after the other, but, though there may be some truth in this view, it didn't account for the large number of sensible people who dressed fashionably and attractively.

Specifically, on this particular day, I was thinking about leg warmers, which seemed to be very much the fashion at that time. These little bits of woolly knit ruffled just above the foot looked very attractive to my eye that day. Why should this be? They certainly didn't draw the eye to or accentuate the usual areas of female anatomy associated with desire. Surely even those Victorians opposed to bare ankles would have no cause for complaint against leg warmers... and yet... well... they were undeniably sexy. Of course this is another example of knowledge and desire in operation. The knowledge is the perception of beauty or attractiveness—what I was calling at that time 'a complex set of universals'—accompanied by actual attraction or desire which I had come to recognise as 'spiritual'; either of demonic, human, angelic or Holy Spirit origin... or some combination, tension or battle of these.

In my thoughts that day, I continued by comparing anointing that accompanies preaching or worship with the 'anointing' that seemed to be in the latest fashion. Certain worship songs carry an anointing for a time and then seem to drop out of 'fashion' and no longer have that special 'coolness' or 'cache'. Even the language we use supports the comparison I was making.

Just after arriving at this point in my thoughts, I began to have a great desire for the colour red. I could perceive it in my spirit very clearly and it seemed very attractive and beautiful—I could almost taste it. I knew it was a desire from God—an anointing from the Holy Spirit—a desire of the Spirit for 'red'. I didn't know what to make of this but knew God was showing me something about his involvement in the fashion scene. I briefly prayed for the release of 'red'. Then my thoughts moved on to something else, but I bore the experience in mind.

A few months later, there was a short period where red became a very 'in fashion' colour especially for accessories like belts, bags and scarves and sometimes trim and edging on coats... and one of my colleagues even greatly desired and bought a red Bible during that period. I conclude that God gets into fashion and has his own influence there. He is the inventor of beauty, and the crown of his creation is supposed to be beautiful, not only in hidden inner ways, but just plain beautiful for all to see.

The folly in our hearts sometimes associates beauty only with sexual attraction, as if sexual intercourse was the only fulfilment of the desire that accompanies beauty. When the Holy Spirit anoints and clothes with beauty, it is for the purpose of love and delight. Sex is part of that within the special context of marriage but to appreciate beauty in all people is also a gift from God, and when He begins to open our eyes, we see more and more beauty. That beauty can, by the Holy Spirit, motivate us to truly love others from the heart; it becomes a pleasure to love and serve. If we find lust rising in our hearts, we need to overcome it, not by avoiding beauty or covering women in religious garments (burkas or habits, for example), but by 'staring it in the face' (so to speak) and letting our hearts be healed and filled with the love of God by the Holy Spirit.

True beauty is the greatest antidote to wrong desire because it is intrinsic to God himself; He created male and female in His own image. It is right and holy for men and women to be attracted to each other—the sin comes from what we do with it, including our thoughts of course, as Jesus warned. But, the appreciation and delight in beauty is not the same as lust; it is actually the opposite. Several times the Holy Spirit has appeared to me as a woman so beautiful and free that every ugly and unloving thought finds no place at all. For this reason, we should all be as beautiful as we can be, and though I know there are certain fashions motivated by evil, I also know there are many motivated by the Holy Spirit and the holy angels of God.

If the devil had total control of fashion, there would be no beauty at all. He would shroud everyone in baggy and drab greens and blues like the communists, or 'shapeless sacks' like some 'religions' do. And he would cover not only the heads and faces of women, but men and children too. For it is the beautiful light from the face of Jesus and the face of the Father, shining through human faces, that offends and frightens him most.

In conclusion: Be beautiful and bless the world with

heavenly beauty. And, why not be open to the Holy Spirit leading in intercession for the fashion scene? The Holy Spirit brought the desire for 'red' that day because he was teaching me how 'heavenly hydraulics' operate into the world through knowledge and desire. If fashion interests you, ask Him, and he will connect you with the power of heaven, to bring the beauty of heaven even into the darkest fashion centres on earth.

## Architecture

On another day during my first year in London, I was walking through residential streets past the old houses and I began to think about why, in former times, houses were made with lots of decorative detail like bay windows framed by pillars capped with sculptured fruit and flowers. It didn't make sense. In those days there were few power tools and no computers. All of the mouldings and decoration would be much easier for us to make today and yet we build everything in the plainest, dullest, utilitarian way. Why? I set the question before the Lord.

Bear in mind I had grown up in the sixties and seventies, which were the veritable depths of utilitarian architecture; and even in the early eighties, when I was first in London, the dull and the dreary were the order of the day. Remember too that during this period my main direction in prayer and warfare was in connection with WWII and the effect that had had on London.

A few days after my first thoughts about architectural beauty, I had a dentist appointment, and while sitting in the waiting room, I happened to pick up a magazine with an article: 'The Architecture of Adolf Hitler'. 'Limestone horrors' is how the writer described the oddly proportioned boxes that passed for buildings in Mr Hitler's eyes. I knew in my spirit that, in addition to the utilitarianism necessitated by war, a diabolical will lay behind the architectural ugliness of the war and post-war period. The cold war communists had taken this to an even greater extreme, actually destroying old buildings with craftsmanship and beauty in them and replacing them with buildings very much in the 'Hitler style'. Again, this is an example of knowledge and desire in operation. The universal—as abstracted by my mind from the architectural details (plain concrete boxes)—was 'ugliness'; which is evidently attended by its own diabolical desire... or, in my heart, repulsion.

This diabolical desire from the Nazis—this demon—had been released onto the Soviet Communists (to a great degree because they rejected God's help) and onto the Western Allies (to a lesser degree because of prayer) through the conflict with the spirit of Nazi Germany. Let no one be so foolish and deceived as to believe, that a demonic power such as Hitler and the Nazis had, can be overcome by guns and bombs and political will, without the help of God!

My prayer in this was part of the help God had provided... and was still providing, against the spirit released through the war. The Holy Spirit inspires desire for beauty, which in this context pertained to architectural detail: pleasingly blended pillars, motifs from nature, curves, domes, peaks and many similar things. The burden of this 'beauty against ugliness' began to settle on my heart, and I knew I wasn't just an observer, but a participant in something God wanted to do. Later that week, at the Sunday evening worship, it was heavy on me like a huge pillar standing on and in my heart. Out of the worship of the whole congregation, a power far beyond what my heart could have borne seemed to flow through the pillar from our meeting all the way to heaven into which the pillar extended. I knew something very consequential was shifting in the heavens and on earth that night; architectural 'fashion' was in flux.

A few days later I received a confirming token. At the Thursday team meeting, one of the ICF leaders, Ray Mayhew, shared that as he had taken the train up to London earlier in the week, he had felt a sense of oppression lifting off the blocks of council flats that he could see through the train window. There was little other evidence of change on the short term, but in following years architectural trends moved significantly in the direction of beauty and craftsmanship. During the later eighties, you might even say, there was a neo-Victorian revival across the whole Western world.

As for the flats that Ray had mentioned, many were demolished to thin out the estates to a more reasonable and pleasant density and flat roofs were replaced with peaks. The lifting of oppression seemed to correspond to city planners and architects beginning to recognise that architecture is closely linked to a sense of belonging and well-being.

And me? ...well, I know that the devil likes everything ugly; and God likes everything beautiful.

## Music

The National Centre for Orchestral Studies ran a course and held classes and practice sessions at The Greenwich Borough Hall, near the area in which I worked. One of the violinists from this course was in our congregation and invited me to an afternoon rehearsal session for a Tchaikovsky concerto they were performing that evening. Having thoughts about 'access' at the forefront of my mind at the time, I light-heartedly asked God for access into the music. My vague thought was, 'I wonder how far you can go into the music?'

I relaxed and closed my eyes and stepped into it. I passed through the music, came to a bleak empty room, and found myself face to face with the composer: Tchaikovsky himself. Being fresh from my encounter with the Victorian Baptist pastor (from the New Life Centre), I explained the gospel to him—expecting resistance because of that previous experience. Tchaikovsky, however, immediately bowed in repentance. I opened my eyes and enjoyed the rest of the performance.

Music and all the arts are spiritual doorways, and part of the angelic-demonic battleground the Holy Spirit can lead us into. In the same way worship songs may fluctuate in the level of anointing they carry because the anointing is fiercely contested by religious spirits in a battle most acutely felt by worship leaders and songwriters. Old songs that have lost their 'edge' can be resurrected if an anointed leader picks them up in the guidance of the Holy Spirit and rereleases them. For intercessors and prophets and worship leaders, the sky is literally the limit here: Why not have some adventures with God and see what could happen?

## Philosophy and Academia: John Wycliffe

At some point in my year of training in church planting, and in the midst of forming my understanding of spiritual dwelling places as 'motifs of knowledge' or 'universals'—though I was just developing that vocabulary—I came across a dismissive reference in a biography of John Wycliffe (1330-1384, sometimes called the Morningstar of the reformation) to the effect that he had written philosophically on the 'reality of universal conceptions'. My spiritual ears perked up—not least because I found the book and the author's tone very annoying. Surely, anything this author thought was irrelevant was in truth the interesting bit he had left out!

I was aware of how each generation needs to 'reopen the

wells' or recover the knowledge of the past in its full spiritual significance. True spiritual knowledge is in constant battle. Statements about God and his ways lose their 'prophetic edge' and need to be understood and taught again in every generation because the anointing and understanding on true words is fiercely contested. Jesus' only reference to the 'key of knowledge', *'Woe to you lawyers! for you have taken away the key of knowledge; you did not enter yourselves, and you hinder those who were entering'* (Luke 11:52), is in the negative. This is because the normal state of play on planet earth is that the gate of true knowledge has been blocked up by the very people ('lawyers'—interpreters of scripture; teachers and theologians) commissioned to keep it open.

This is why Jesus' teachings often involved reopening the truths of the Old Testament. Similarly, in every generation, the teachings of Jesus, the teachings of the Apostles, and teachings from key eras in church history need to be reopened; like the wells of Abraham that Isaac had to re-dig. (Ref: Genesis 26:18) This is the normal battle with the religious spirit that we are all involved with whether we want to be or not.

And so, I decided to find the connection between Wycliffe's theology and philosophy and life: they had to be integrated if he was a genuine man of God. That is to say, if he was one who—unlike the lawyers whom Jesus rebuked—*did* enter himself, and therefore *helps* rather than 'hinders those who were entering'. The key of true knowledge is given to those who enter; to those who walk in love and obedience.

*The Gates of Eden*

It is hard even to recall nowadays how difficult it was in pre-Internet 1983-4 to open a comprehensive study on Wycliffe. Every reference to Wycliffe in Christian writing ignored his philosophy, and his philosophy in academia had long since fallen out of vogue. Even a friend reading philosophy at Oxford knew nothing about it; though Wycliffe had arguably been the university's brightest star in his century, and his legacy in the translation of scriptures, the Lollard Movement, and the reformation stand him among the most consequential men of England's—indeed the world's—history.

Fortunately I was able to take a few days as a research student at the old British Library reading room. I ordered every book attributed to Wycliffe, and a steward with white gloves brought them to me (some things were better before the Internet). Some of the books were ancient and falling apart—supplied in plastic bags; others were newer, only a century or two old. I soon discovered the volume I was looking for: *Tractatus de Universalibus* .

Unfortunately, it had never been translated from its original Latin, though it had been edited and annotated by a scholar of the Wycliffe society, circa 1900. I gleaned bits and pieces from this and also learned that the original work had only been preserved because Jan Huss (1369-1415, often seen as a pre-reformer alongside Wycliffe) had a copy of it at the University of Prague when Wycliffe's bones were dug up and burned along with his books and papers in England. The connection between Huss and Wycliffe had evidently covered academic philosophy, and not just theology, as I had previously imagined.

Not only was Wycliffe's philosophy still in Latin in 1983-84, but it was all written in difficult Scholastic Medieval Latin—which C. S. Lewis called 'impenetrable Latin'. I thought, 'If C. S. Lewis, who was fluent in classic Latin found Wycliffe's Latin impenetrable, what hope is there for me?' And isn't it perversely ironic that Wycliffe, whose name is associated so strongly with translation of the Bible into English, should himself be thus concealed in a lost language? So I said to God, 'Please get someone to translate this book (Wycliffe's *Tractatus de Universalibus*) for me.'

About that time, or probably even before (though I didn't find out until a year or two later), Anthony Kenny, who was then 63rd master at Balliol College, Oxford—same college where Wycliffe had been 13th master—decided to mark the 600th anniversary of Wycliffe's death (1384) by translating *Tractatus de Universalibus* into English. Kenny, having been a Catholic priest prior to taking up an academic career specialising in mediaeval philosophy, was probably one of the few people on the planet capable of the feat. That he was from Wycliffe's old college is a bit of God's serendipitous 'class'. And for a bit of God's own irony: Anthony Kenny, after leaving Catholicism, had become an agnostic; and two of the world's most famous atheists, Richard Dawkins and Christopher Hitchens, had been students at Balliol College. It doesn't seem the most likely place for God to get a look-in, never mind a job done, but I guess He has a sense of humour. In any case, sometime in 1986, I had the book, *On Universals*, in my hands.

*The Gates of Eden*

So it was happy endings all around? Hardly! The book was almost as impenetrable in English as it had been in Latin—even Kenny himself didn't claim to be able to follow Wycliffe's line of reasoning in many cases. Indeed, it is doubtful that the mysteries of spiritual dwelling places in knowledge and the warfare surrounding them can be penetrated by philosophy and logic alone; though I suspect Huss and Wycliffe had gone further on this than we have yet recovered in our age. One thing I do know from this experience is that God can give access into the academic world and every realm of knowledge. Indeed, part of the end-times glory will be the recovery of wisdom, revelation and knowledge from every era of the history of God's people.

One helpful thing I learned about Wycliffe from Anthony Kenny (see his: 'Wycliffe' in the Oxford 'Past Masters' series) is that he was not the 'Calvinistic Predestinarian' that some claim he was; but rather more in the Hus and Luther line of thinking. The peril of being a hero, or even a villain, is that of being claimed incorrectly and linked to various causes in subsequent centuries. Joan of Arc, for example, has been optimistically latched onto by everyone from communists to gays to feminists; and in antithesis, Adolf Hitler has been the persecutor of every cause that wants a share in that glorious credential. (It's always good to keep a 'grain of salt' at hand when it comes to this kind of thing!)

[Note: I have included an appendix where I discuss some of the philosophy that Wycliffe was grappling with in his time. It is relevant to the question of knowledge and spiritual dwelling places, but too large a digression to include here. A second appendix, 'The Armour of Ghostly Battle', brings a flavour of Wycliffe's later preaching, as well as his pastoral heart. It is also still helpful and relevant to prayer and spiritual warfare.]

## A Note of Caution

The main thing in this area of 'access'—the 'gates of the earth'—is to stay in the anointing of the Holy Spirit with our eyes on the Father because it is through our access to Him that any authority can be exerted on the earth. There is no point in having access on earth if we don't have the power to do anything about it. Without the living dynamic access to the Father's face in the Holy Spirit, we are powerless and likely only to come under oppression if we do gain earthly access. Earthly knowledge, earthly positions of leadership and other earthly power can provide earthly access, but what on earth will you do with it if you don't have access to the Father in heaven?

About five years after the experiences mentioned in this book, an emphasis on 'spiritual mapping' and 'territorial spirits' became very popular in the church worldwide—sometimes beyond the Spirit's leading. There is nothing wrong with these perspectives in themselves, but if we get out of step with Father and the Holy Spirit, we are vulnerable to confusion, lack of focus and enemy ambush, which leads to failure and frustration. Because that happened in some cases, the pendulum of Christian thinking has swung hard in the opposite direction, so now, as I'm writing, in 2014, we need to recover the truths of knowledge and desire and access in spiritual warfare—including territorial strongholds—all over again.

Let us be wise to stay in the Spirit this time and not turn it all into another religious technique. In the 'fog of war', the main thing is to keep a clear line of communication with the commander in chief. There is only one Lord of the Harvest. He alone has the overview, wisdom and power. Let us be like the servant whose eyes are on the master's hands and the handmaiden whose eyes are always on the hands of her mistress (Ref: Psalm123.2); in the words of Jesus: '*... only what he sees the Father doing; for whatever he does, that the son does likewise.*' (John5:19)

## CHAPTER 5
# WWII AND THE CROSS: GATE OF HOPE AND GLORY

*'...Christ in you, the hope of glory.'*
(Colossians 1:27)

### AN OLD DESIRE

In the way that C. S. Lewis spoke of desiring 'northernness' and 'autumn' in his book *Surprised by Joy,* I had long desired, with joy and sorrow, what I imagined to be the WWII atmosphere of London. I had no idea that this was a desire from the Holy Spirit when it first occurred—I never analysed it at all—it was just one of those things that seems to roll into the life of a happy, inquisitive child. It came through a schoolbook when I was in the third or fourth grade—about eight or nine years old. The book, full of large colourful pictures, told the story of a young woman who worked in a paint factory that was bombed one night during the blitz. More than the story, the pictures brought to my heart something of the fear, desperation and deep significance—all coupled with a sense of camaraderie—as everyone pitched in to fight the fire. The young heroine's beautiful and determined face was lit up by the flames against the night sky background; and into the foreground, streams of green, yellow, blue and red paint flowed out from great vats in the burning factory. This picture etched images and desires into my soul which remain to this day.

It seems to me now that this picture was a window to the face of the Holy Spirit, fighting the war, and always at war, against every form of darkness and oppression. Was the Holy Spirit there on those dark wartime nights rallying the people to stand strong together? I think so. This could explain why so many people in 1983, when I first moved to London, still looked at that era as a positive defining period in their lives. Any time I spoke to an older person about anything beyond small talk, the conversation would move—often with nostalgic longing—back to the worst days of the war.

Of course they were terrible times and people could seldom articulate why they longed for them. Sometimes they felt a bit guilty; perhaps they felt themselves the odd one out for having such thoughts. Usually they mentioned the strong sense of community and belonging—after all, surely the war itself was an evil thing. I now believe that it was the heart of God and the tangible presence of the Holy Spirit they were hankering after.

One thing is certain: at the sharp end of every war against evil and darkness, the Holy Spirit can be found. The Holy Spirit of the New Testament era is no fragile dove ready to flee at the first sniff of conflict. No, indeed: he is the Spirit of Jesus and the Spirit of our Heavenly Father; mighty man of war; Lord of Hosts (armies); the finger of

God casting out the devil; and the power by which *'the ruler of this world is judged.'* (John 16:11) He is glorified in Jesus' resurrection and ascension, and neither hovers at a safe distance nor leaves the scene of battle. He dives in to win, and if you find yourself out of step it is probably because you have shrunk back in fear, rather than dived in with Him. It is interesting and instructive to note that, from the day the Holy Spirit descended as a dove and *remained* upon Jesus, as observed by John the Baptist (Ref: John 1:32), He never again appears as a dove in the scriptures—you will not see the dove now, unless you look deeply into the eyes of Jesus.

When I arrived back in London in September 1983, joined the Ichthus Network Course, the Luis Palau 'Mission to London', and church planting in Greenwich, I was soon caught up in a 'war' on the war. God led me through many people and situations into a fulfilment of that desire he had placed in my heart all those years before. Much of the decline in the church and loss of faith among the people of God was the result of their hurts from the terrible things they had experienced during the war. Many—perhaps even most—of that generation had lost loved ones, neighbours and friends. If that seems contradictory to what I said above, such was the feeling in the hearts of people too. Though they hankered back, they were also angry at God and blamed him, as people so often do, for 'letting' such evil things happen.

The fact that he was there with them, sharing the sorrows, is a connection we all need help to make. Just as I never realised that the desires I had were from the Spirit, people seldom realise that the comfort they remember and the desire they feel is because of the Holy Spirit. They don't recognise him, because he is so gentle and unreligious—he is in fact what everyone wished he was like, but can't dare believe he actually *is* like.

A lot of bad theology and dreary church experience has caused this confusion. God is given terrible press, often by those who claim to be his representatives, and of course by the devil: ancient lying serpent and original propagandist. The confusion about God's nature and character is such that people do not recognise him as God when he is right there helping them. We shouldn't be surprised by this—it is exactly what Jesus experienced in first-century Palestine. The work of the evangelist is to dispel lies and bring the truth about God to light, so that people's eyes are opened to see Him and recognise Him as the one who has always loved and cared for them—the one who stood with them in their darkest hours.

Spiritual warfare and prayer are essential to breaking the power of the lies because, even if we win theological debates, people won't necessarily get free. Losing an argument usually just makes people angry unless the spiritual powers of darkness are broken from their eyes at the same time. No doubt, God could win every argument, but he is always more interested in winning hearts, which is why we must follow in Jesus' footsteps, spending time in prayer as well as evangelism. Evangelist Reinhard Bonnke compares prayer and evangelism to detonator and explosive—each ineffective without the other.

And of course prayer is not just another 'thing we must do'. It must be our life and connection with God himself. If we aren't in this tangible dynamic connection, and therefore flowing in the love of God when we speak to people, they will immediately sense we are mere salesmen, trying to please superiors, meet targets or get new members—with money or personal success as our underlying motive. If, however, we carry the very Spirit they themselves hanker after from their own past experiences, we will be able to love and minister to people at the level of their deepest desires and hopes.

## Ron

One of the early events of the Luis Palau Mission to London was a prayer and envisioning meeting for people from the supporting churches at Greenwich Borough Hall. I took the opportunity to talk to one of the stewards, an employee of Greenwich Council named Ron who was probably in his late fifties. He told me he hadn't gone to church since before the war when he had been part of a youth group in Rye Lane Baptist Church in Peckham. He said his youth leader, Stan, had been the only person he had ever known who he thought really lived a true Christian life. While Ron was part of that group, besides having a lot of fun with such things as seaside camp-outs, he felt he had known Jesus. But that was all a long time ago and everything had gone wrong after Stan went to war. Ron's family home had been bombed and they had moved several miles away and he had never seen Stan again—indeed, didn't even know if he was still alive. He became quite tearful as he told me this and I knew Jesus wanted to do something for him.

I remembered an old Canadian children's story about frozen voices. In that story (pure fiction of course), an exceptionally cold winter had caused voices to freeze so that the words were held in cryonic suspension until spring when everything that had been said all winter could at last be heard. The war had been like that cold winter, with relationships—conversations, as it were—frozen up in midstream. But this was a time of spring and it was the will of God that some of those words should thaw.

'Would you like to speak to Stan again?' I asked.

'Yes... but... a lot of men didn't make it back from Germany.'

'I'll find out,' I said, and Ron gave me a doubtful—almost fearful—look. Perhaps he dreaded to finally hear, just as a man might fear to open a pile of post that he suspects is mostly bills.

Next day I headed out to Peckham on my motorcycle and called in at Rye Lane Baptist Church. I was able to get a phone number for Stan's brother who was now a deacon, and through him I got an address. Indeed, Stan hadn't made it back from Germany—but not because he'd been killed; he had fallen in love with a German girl! Now, almost forty years later, I wrote a letter to him, and gave him Ron's address. He wrote to us both and arranged to meet Ron on his next trip to London. Ron never did join the congregation I was planting in Greenwich, but I dropped in on him a few times at the Borough Hall and he said he prayed again now and knew that Jesus was still in his life.

## Brian and the Gates of Hades

Brian's story is not one worth telling if superficial triumph and success are the only criteria. Despite great effort on my part, he never found his way out of the quagmire his life had descended into. However, God still used him and his situation to teach me some valuable lessons and he was a doorway into demonic strongholds in the area. He was truly a lost soul. A life of drink and drugs and reckless immorality in his youth and early adulthood had been followed by a heartbreaking series of live-in partners in his thirties and forties. By the time I met him in his fifties, his physical and mental health was gone, and outwardly he looked as dirty and dishevelled as he seemed inwardly. He pined over long-lost girlfriends with hopeless pathos.

An initial connection with him came my way because he had gone forward for prayer at the end of a Mission to London tent meeting. As he was in my area, I was assigned the follow-up and soon found myself in frontline spiritual warfare against spiritualism. Brian claimed to be the grandson of a famous spiritualist of the late Victorian era.

I never verified this part of his story but had no reason to doubt it. Indeed, I have often observed the connection between spiritualism and heartbreak in relationships, including untimely deaths, physical and mental sickness, and diverse other tragedies. In praying for people who had touched into spiritualism, I noticed a recurring pattern: every word given by a spiritualist or fortune teller contained negative statements about existing or future relationships. The enemy's words are discernible by their negative fruit: pain and death—his words are poison. Conversely, the words of God release life and health.

One day, I felt great concern when my co-worker had gone down to Brian's house for a visit while I was on my way to another meeting. I prayed briefly for protection and saw in the spirit a very large angel standing near the house. The angel stood as high as the smoke stacks of the old Greenwich power station, also there beside the Thames and only a few hundred yards from Brian's house. I knew my co-worker was safe but the vision of the angel remained with me. As I continued looking, I began to see that the angel, though providing protection and shining light all around him, was bound to the earth by what appeared to be huge concrete bases or clamps. I remembered the words from Revelation 9:14 *'Release the four angels who are bound at the great river Euphrates.'* I had a spiritual 'itch' to proclaim release to this angel and so I began to speak it out: 'Release the great angel bound by the river Thames!'

As I took this call up in prayer, my understanding was opened to something of the angelic demonic battle going on in the heavens. I knew that this particular angel had been bound through the activities of spiritualists—unwittingly perhaps—but destructive and damaging to ordinary folk all the same. 'High priests' of spiritualism like Brian's grandfather had been responsible for this angel being bound in that place for over a hundred years. My vision of this bound angel was a representative view of the spiritual stronghold that had been established through spiritualism in London.

The battle over spiritualism raged on for several years after this and we saw many salvations as a result of victories—though Brian himself never came through. He made some progress for a while but as soon as he was together enough to attract (or entrap) a new girlfriend, he went around the same cycle of pain and heartbreak all over again. However, despite his personal unwillingness to change, the stronghold in the area was shifting.

A day came perhaps two years later when the whole congregation—about sixty people by that time—had a praise march from east Greenwich to central Greenwich, right past Brian's neighbourhood, and where the angel was bound. An elderly retired missionary in the congregation (mentioned earlier), herself having been wounded by spiritualism through her family's response to a brother lost during the war, came to me with what she described as overwhelming visions. She had seen in the spirit a large host of people from the past marching through Greenwich, just as the congregation had marched. They were dressed in the styles of earlier periods and seemed to be coming out of bondage into freedom. I knew it related to the angel and that a great host of people from the past were coming into freedom along with the angel. When I walked through the area later that day, I saw only the broken shackles left behind in the place where the angel had been bound for more than a century.

Certainly one lesson to draw from this is that God uses our prayers and labour to accomplish great things even if the specific thing we are praying and working for doesn't happen. Brian himself never did choose freedom, but he was still a doorway into a stronghold in the area, which was used to bring other people into freedom. Hosea spoke of this kind of access or gate when he prophesied: *'And I will give her her vineyards, and make the Valley of Achor a door of hope.'* (Hosea 2:15)

While originally this refers to Joshua's 'trouble' (meaning of 'Achor') with the idolatrous man, Achan, at the Valley of Achor, and, in the interim, Hosea's marriage troubles, ultimately it speaks of the cross: the total and perfect turning of troubles into doorways of hope. It speaks of those troublesome gates of Hades, opened against the human race by sin, now being turned into the very avenue to destroy the works of the evil one, by the death and resurrection of Jesus.

Spiritually speaking, Jesus, like a mighty Samson, tore those gates of death from their hinges—bars and all—and carried them to the top of the hill, making a public display of their failure for all to see. (Ref: Judges 16:3; Colossians 2:15)

*The Gates of Eden*

## THE QUEST FOR THE UNIFIED FIELD

In the 'Network' training programme, each student had several papers to research and present to one or two of the Ichthus leaders and the rest of the class. My second paper—totally integrated with my warfare about the World War II and the roots of Nazism—was called 'The quest for the Unified Field'.

The unified field is the 'holy grail' of classic philosophy; the union of the 'three transcendentals': beauty, truth and goodness; God: the 'one, good and true'. In physics, unified field theory pertains to integrating two or more of the four primary forces or interactions: gravity, electromagnetic, strong nuclear and weak nuclear. To Christians, it is the God 'in whom we live and move and have our being'; the King and the Kingdom of Heaven.

It was the assertion of that kingdom of heaven into the history of Germany that became my burden at this time. Throughout German history, I noticed two strong strands—one of God's people and the other of evil men. The parallel seemed uncanny. When God raised up a 'Luther', a 'Faust' was near at hand. When God raised up the Moravians at Herrnhut, the enemy raised up Schopenhauer, Feuerbach and the whole school of liberal theology.

The root of this theology in spiritual terms was of greatest interest to me. Schopenhauer's thought was so Vedic Hindu in origin that Will Durant, in his *World History*, snidely described the Hindu philosophy (actually of course from several thousand years before Schopenhauer) as: 'More Schopenhaueren than Schopenhauer.' This theology was a doctrine of demons inhabited by demons, and one of the main powers of the darkness that overcame the German people during the nineteenth century and into the twentieth, ultimately, in its maturity, empowering Adolf Hitler and the Nazis.

Besides the 'theology', the Prussian eagle, which became the standard emblem of Hitler's army, also originated in this ancient Vedic Hindu religion. The bird of prey and the counsel of Schopenhauer and co. are the 'fingerprints' of the demonic stronghold that deceived the German people. (The swastika also has strong links to ancient Hinduism.)

In the Holy Spirit and God's great hydraulic system, I stepped into the biblical paradigm of, *'My counsel shall stand, and I will accomplish all my purpose, calling a bird of prey from the east, and a man of my counsel from a far country.'* (Isaiah 46:10-11) Ultimately, it was a conflict of 'counsels'; of two systems of 'knowledge', with the cross of Christ, greatest love and tree on Mount Calvary, ever prevailing over the serpent's tree of the knowledge of good and evil!

Within the compass of the serpent's tree are found not just this bit of religion and philosophy that deceived the Germans, but all false philosophy and religion. On the other hand, in the great tree at Golgotha—the cross of Jesus—the counsels of heaven establish the purposes of God; namely the total victory of love (though apparently weak), and the absolute failure of all evil (though evidently powerful).

*'For the word of the cross is folly to those who are perishing, but to us who are being saved it is the power of God. For it is written, "I will destroy the wisdom of the wise, and the cleverness of the clever I will thwart." Where is the wise man? Where is the scribe? Where is the debater of this age? Has not God made foolish the wisdom of the world? For since, in the wisdom of God, the world did not know God through wisdom; it pleased God through the folly of what we preach to save those who believe. For Jews demand signs and Greeks seek wisdom, but we preach Christ crucified, a stumbling block to Jews and folly to Gentiles, but to those who are called, both Jews and Greeks, Christ the power of God and the wisdom of God. For the foolishness of God is wiser than men, and the weakness of God is stronger than men.'* (I Corinthians 1:18-25)

## THE CROSS AND THE WAR

One of the books on the Networkers' 'required reading' list was Norman Grubb's biography of Rees Howells, the Welsh intercessor who had been powerfully used by God before and during the war. This book was a trigger in bringing a whole new dimension of prayer and intercession into operation in my own life. For one thing, it brought the paradox of the cross more sharply into focus; the point of seeming total defeat being the actual point of total victory was coming very alive in my spirit—sometimes it seemed that I was standing on the very brink of limitless faith. Every bad thing could be transformed into victory in the penetrating search light—the shocking power in apparent weakness—of the cross.

I had this reinforced for me one day during the early weeks of working in East Greenwich. I was doing some 'pub evangelism' at a pub called 'The Ship and Billet' (now 'The Duchess Wine Bar'). I struck up a conversation with an old man, who was quite drunk, and began to explain to him how Jesus' death on the cross and resurrection opened the door for us to become children of God, and gave us power to change our lives.

'I believe God guides my steps,' he said in a heavily slurred voice. 'Every night when I leave this pub I can hardly walk but somehow I always make it home.' I reflected briefly on this statement of faith, but before I had arrived at any conclusions, he continued, 'I believe in Jesus on the cross too. One night during the war, I was walking home in Rotherhithe when a bomb hit a church. The whole building came down and the only thing left standing was Jesus on the cross—with rubble all around.'

I saw the image in my own mind as if I was standing there with him that night and I knew God was speaking something into my own heart. It was a word of faith to me. In all the destruction and devastation of the church because of the war, Jesus on the cross still stood over it all and every loss and failure could, in the power of his resurrection, be turned to good. This word became like an engine of faith in my heart over the following weeks and the feeling of standing on the brink of limitless faith was intensifying daily.

It was during this period that I had an experience of seeing an old man in Norway, coming out of his woodshed prayer closet circa 1800. I believe this was one of my ancestors who had, in his time, prophetically seen forward to my time and surrounded in prayer some of the issues in Germany that were only embryonic in 1800, but came to fruition in the Nazis and WWII. There was such a beautiful feeling as our eyes met and the connection was made, of entering a fellowship in prophetic prayer across time. This bridging of generations and time itself is intrinsic to the eternal redemption that Jesus secured when he offered his own 'blood of the eternal covenant' in the 'eternal Spirit'. (Ref: Hebrews 9:12-14; 13:20)

**The cross, properly understood in the Holy Spirit, is eternally effective and immediately powerful in every moment of time. The power of the cross has never been confined to the first century, but saturates time from the foundation of the world to the eternal future. It is God's love, eternally active and alive, as it is prayed, believed, and preached in every generation.**

In the power of the cross, a day came when I thought I could actually step across into limitless faith—but I don't really know what that was... It seemed like a gateway into a different 'dimension'. As I stood there at that 'spiritual junction' or 'gate', the Lord said to me, 'If you lay this down, you can have it for all the congregations.' In the tenderness of that moment I never hesitated to let it go. It was hardly a choice, because of his presence, and I'm not sure of all that it means to this day. One thing is certain:

though there are many different times and seasons within the harvest and in our lives, there is only one who is *Lord* of the harvest, and he alone has the overview and wisdom to manage it all.

## CHAPTER 6
# TRANSTEMPORAL INTERCESSION: GATES OF THE AGES

After the choice to give back to God the opportunity or doorway into—what had at least seemed to me—limitless faith, I began to move into a new depth and complexity in spiritual warfare. Though I never made the connection at the time, the Spirit now witnesses to my heart that this was one of the results of my choice. For this reason, and because it connects many strands I've been speaking about so far, I will recount here something I consider to be one of the most significant prayer battles of the period.

On a certain Friday of each month the fellowship had a half night of prayer which the networkers were expected to attend. It was led at the time by Roger Mitchell (a member of the ICF leadership team) who also headed up the network course. On this particular night, probably the 20th of January 1984, Roger had it on his heart to pray for six particular people from the first Ichthus 'extension area' or new congregation which was in lower Sydenham. That congregation had been planted only a year or two earlier and spiritual breakthroughs there were seen as crucial for breakthrough in other congregations as well. He listed the six people who had all been early converts in that congregation but who had subsequently fallen away for one reason or another.

As we began praying for these six people, I had a vision of a large ship and my attention was drawn to six large cable pulleys on the forward deck. I don't know the correct nautical term for these pulleys, but they are the ones that rotate in the horizontal plane and are perhaps used to tighten the lines that are attached to the dock when the ship is in port. I couldn't make a lot of sense of the picture—I don't know if any real ship has six of these pulleys—but I knew the pulleys in some way related to the six people. I also knew God was putting it on my heart to pray for these people.

The next morning I was up early and, in the kitchen of Ichthus house where I lived, made myself some toast and tea. Just as I was spreading marmalade on the toast, the Lord said to me, 'I want you to fast for six days starting right now.' Now, normally we all love to hear the Lord speak but when he says something like that, we are inclined to have second thoughts. 'Is this really the Lord or just some religious vibe?' is usually my first response if it's something I don't feel like doing. 'I can't waste this food I've prepared' was my lame response on this occasion. Then I immediately thought of a homeless man whom I knew to be sleeping in the outer porch of the parish church which was only a few hundred metres from Ichthus house. 'But I'm not allowed to give food from Ichthus house to the poor—I have to buy food myself if

I want to do that.' The Lord dismissed my legalistic interpretation of this rule with a kind but weary glance. And so I poured my tea into a polystyrene cup, made my fresh toast into a sandwich, wrapped it in foil and took it to the tramp. He had not been planning to rise quite so early, but received it thankfully all the same.

## MOSES, PAUL AND ISRAEL'S DESTINY

Throughout this process, almost at another level of consciousness, I was aware of the ship and pulleys I had seen in the vision the night before—which I could still see. I was also aware that the Lord wanted to make a connection in the spiritual realm between the martyrs of WWII including the six million Jews killed by the Nazis and also all the soldiers because it says in Isaiah 14:19, in speaking of the judgement of the king of Babylon and Lucifer, that he will be: '...*clothed with the slain, those pierced by the sword ...*' The blood of those killed in the war had begun to weigh heavily on my soul for some time at this point and part of the intercession was to bring a claim before the throne of God for the blood of martyrs—especially on this occasion—the six million Jews.

For some weeks before this, I had become aware of a realm of intercession where there is a connection across the generations in one great spiritual war that will consummate in the final casting down of the devil and the return of Christ and his kingdom on earth. (My understanding of this, as it has developed over the years, can be found in some of my other writings such as *The Mantles of Jesus*.) In regard to the blood of the Jews killed by Hitler, I became aware of the intercession of the Apostle Paul and Moses who both reached a point where they were willing to sacrifice not just their physical lives, but even their own place in God's book—that is, eternal life. The power of these intercessions, along with others, are kept in bowls in Heaven (as pictured by John in Rev5:8) ready to be poured out at the time the Lord of the Harvest chooses to do so.

I could feel the power of those intercessions, in the past, and of the need to bring them forward. Somehow in the middle of it all was my ship with the six pulleys. I searched for a way to connect the power through them. The Spirit carried me back to a day when I was a child with my father at the grain elevator in town where we hauled our grain from the farm. As a curious little boy, I was looking into a small open doorway, at a drive belt that ran from the stationary engine in the room behind the office to the main elevator where it drove a vertical conveyor system that lifted the grain to the top of the elevator. I asked my dad what it was and he explained it to me.

Somehow his explanation had placed in my spirit the essence of that belt—the very atmosphere from seeing that powerful belt through that dark little doorway was alive in my spirit—so much so that I could feel the slight wind it stirred up against my face as I stood in that place between times in the spiritual realm. This was another instance of my natural father being a window to the heavenly Father. Every moment we spend and every word we speak to our children is potentially eternally precious—even, as in this case, a seemingly ordinary explanation of a mechanical device.

Each day I fasted I was able to take a belt from that memory and connect the power from the past intercessions of Paul and Moses and extend them forward into the future—into darkness, as it were. I could see the ship with drive belts coming from the past, going around the six pulleys, which then drove belts that extended into the unknown—the future; the salvation of all the Jews. The intercessions of the past were somehow blended with the blood of the wartime martyrs and great power was sent into some future era, which was hidden from my eyes.

During the last days of the fast, I was under a constant barrage from the enemy and very tempted to end the fast. On the Thursday, which was the sixth day, I was at the leadership team meeting, which that day happened to be in the building used by the congregation in lower Sydenham where the six people were originally from. I said to the Lord, 'I need a 'six' from you to confirm I'm actually meant to continue for the full six days.' After a period of worship, Roger Forster, leader of the fellowship, gave a short teaching around the text *'making the most of the time, because the days are evil.'* (Ephesians 5:16) He likened every day to a cricket ball with the potential to knock the wicket and put the batter out. But each day was also a ball that could be hit by the batter—to score a Six. (I knew nothing of cricket but inferred that a six was the maximum points for a hit.) As he was reiterating his point, he paused just before saying 'six' and Roger Mitchell, sitting on the front row, chimed in with his great baritone voice: 'SIX.' Even later, I began to wonder if I had just made this up and so listened to the tape—which clearly picked up this 'SIX'. And so I had the encouragement I needed to persevere through the last day.

I've included this bit of the story to give a glimpse of the kind of interactive 'coincidences' that were a daily occurrence in the Ichthus Fellowship in those days. This kind of unity and flow in the Spirit is the context where high-level spiritual warfare can take place and where faith can operate far beyond what any individual could attain. *'Behold, how good and pleasant it is when brothers dwell in unity! It is like oil upon the beard, upon the beard of Aaron, running down on the collar of his robes! It is like the dew of Hermon, which falls on the mountains of Zion! For there the Lord has commanded the blessing, life for evermore.'* (Psalm 133:1-3)

After I had finished the fast, I held this vision as a burden in my heart for several years. The power continued to flow and I could look at it in the Spiritual realm whenever I chose but it required no additional prayer or effort. Sometimes the ship seemed to be on very stormy seas but always the belts held and continued conveying great power forward in time. After about four years it faded until it seems, to this day, like an ordinary memory.

If I was to attempt an interpretation, I suppose I would say that a season of revival is coming to the Jews that will be of unprecedented power and that will continue for about four years at great intensity. I know this story sounds beyond flaky even to most charismatic Christians, and completely off the scale of insanity to everyone else, so I won't labour the details. I'm not entirely immune to feeling that things like this are crazy myself, but the Lord is very kind and has always given confirming tokens, which I understand he also did for the prophets—little near-term fulfilments to confirm that I'm on the right track when dealing with something that may be on a much longer scale than my attention span or lifetime. In the passage referred to above, Isaiah prophesied of the ultimate fall of Lucifer and his kingdom of darkness as a parallel to the fall of Babylon, which was a relatively near-term event. I have always looked for similar objective tokens or indicators in conjunction with intercession to keep a reality check against *'...visions, puffed up without reason...'* (Colossians 2:18)

I have often discovered, after intercession like this, that God had many people doing something similar or parallel. I would therefore expect that others, on reading this story, could share their own story. Most of this kind of thing remains hidden, but it is healthy to bear in mind God's word to Elijah, about the 7000 people who never bowed the knee to Baal, and yet were unknown—even to Elijah.

## INDICATORS AND TOKENS

The tokens, or 'indicators' as I like to call them, came in the way appropriate to me and the situation and also confirm that my part in all this was only a small part. There were six people, who corresponded to the six pulleys and whom I had started out praying for after the half night of prayer, but only one I ever heard of again: a married woman in her mid twenties.

Several months after my fasting and prayer, this woman, a backslidden Christian (which is why we had been praying for her in the first place), brought a non-Christian colleague from her workplace to my congregation one Sunday morning. The friend became a Christian (and a few years later my wife—that's another story), but the woman herself went on backsliding and had an affair with a married man. They both eventually divorced their previous spouses and set up home together. One Saturday night, this man, who had no Christian background, had some kind of encounter with God, got up the next morning and announced that he was going to church. They found a local church where he got dramatically saved and she recommitted her life to the Lord. They married and he went on after a few years to become an evangelist and pastor.

God never violates free will but the story of this woman is a sign and an indicator to me of the persistence and determination of the Holy Spirit. In spite of her determination to rebel, she was relentlessly pursued by the Holy Spirit. To do that without violating her free will, God dramatically blessed people around her. This is also an indicator of the nature of the power that was moving in the heavens through my vision of the ship and the drive belts. I believe the events of her life indicate in cameo something of the nature of the revival power that is coming to Israel in the future. (And a whole lot more besides, because she was only one of six people who corresponded to my original vision—not to mention the many other people and churches praying for revival in Israel and the Middle East.)

## CHAPTER 7
# HEART OF LIGHT: BREAKING THE IRON GATE OF RELIGION

### HEALER OF BROKEN HEARTS

A few months into the Network course, though I had felt a lot of breakthrough in prayer and growth in faith, the Lord was still working on my heart. One Sunday night—as mentioned in an earlier chapter—during a worship service at the Dietrich Bonhoeffer Memorial Church, someone had shared a picture of a teardrop falling from the Lord's eye, describing in detail how it fell like a precious diamond with many facets. Someone else gave the interpretation: 'Jesus has brought healing—there is healing in this meeting.'

I was not aware of any need for healing myself but was open-hearted to receive anything the Lord was doing and so simply said yes to his healing. I immediately perceived that some healing had taken place in my heart. I had a little picture of new flesh in place of an old cut or scar, and it gave me a nice warm feeling inside. I didn't know what had been healed; just that it was something in my heart.

My cousin Joanne had dropped in on her way home from Nigeria to Canada for a few days just then, and the following day, which was my day off, we were doing the tourist sites in London. While we were walking around Westminster Abbey, I happened to say just under my breath, and perhaps in reaction to the religious atmosphere, 'I love you, Jesus.' I was shocked because I felt that I really meant it. I had said this to the Lord many times before but never with real faith; never before had I had a real sense that I actually deeply meant it. I knew at once this was because of the healing I had received in the meeting the night before.

Our hearts are like vessels or cups that hold our inner motivations and desires, but when they have wounds, they leak and never maintain the fullness we long for. We have intense feelings that dissipate as quickly as they come: our motivations fade; our good intentions of the evening are cold memories by morning; we fall in love quickly, and out of love even quicker. When they are healed, however, we can say with the Psalmist: *'He restores my soul'* and *'my cup overflows.'* (Psalm 23) The overflowing heart, as opposed to the 'broken cistern that can hold no water', is what we all long for. To be genuine, wholehearted people, who really love—and *feel* that we really love—God and others, rather than just being religious keepers of traditions and ideas, can only come as the deepest places in our hearts are healed by God.

To seek to love God with all our heart, soul, mind and strength will result in receiving his healing love along the way. Ministry training sometimes involves learning the techniques of managing and posturing with what is essentially a broken heart. In the end, this is a very heavy yoke to bear. The reason so many churches are dreary, heartbreaking places is that those who lead them have staggered under this yoke rather than finding that easy, light yoke that Jesus spoke of.

The light yoke of Jesus is borne by those with healed hearts who love him and know it. Such a heart overflows with the beautiful desires of the Spirit, knows the heart of the Father and is at rest in the midst of labours. *'Come to me, all you that labour and are heavy laden and I will give you rest. Take my yoke upon you, and learn of me; for I am gentle and lowly of heart, and you will find rest for your souls. For my yoke is easy, and my burden is light.'* (Matthew 11:28-30) If we seek that gentle and lowly heart, we will surely find it, and in finding it, our own hearts will be healed as well.

## THE CATHOLIC CHURCH

One thing I didn't realise on the day this happened was that it was, like everything God does, a part of a beautiful tapestry or mosaic that he was working in my life. It was no coincidence that I became aware of this healing to my heart at Westminster Abbey, the main Catholic Cathedral in England. Ever since my Christmas experience in Vienna a couple of years earlier, one of the frontiers of God's activity in my life related to the

Catholic Church. I mentioned in my book *The Road to Eden* how, on attending a Mass in Vienna, I had seen a vision of people trapped at the mouth of a cave, whose dark inner precincts seemed to correspond to a deep past that held them in bondage.

The understanding of this vision remained one of the open questions in my heart which God gave answers to at times he deemed appropriate. The reason he doesn't answer some questions immediately is that we don't have enough knowledge to understand any answer he could give. Of all the bondages that trap humans, religion is the most complex and difficult to untangle—and more so when it has entwined itself into governmental authority as well. Even so, all bondages relate ultimately to the heart and the mind, and those who find freedom in the Holy Spirit and the truth from Jesus will be truly free, regardless of external circumstances.

## MARY GRACE

A few months prior to the experience of having my heart healed, I had met a Catholic lady while doing some open-air evangelism with a team in East Dulwich. She was a deeply troubled woman in her early seventies who had had a life of heartache. Now she was tormented by spirits—whether real or psychological is almost irrelevant—and she was in terrible pain and fear. Her name, paradoxically, was Mary Grace. One thing that struck me in speaking to her was how she incorrectly used the first person, 'I', in referring to herself rather than 'me'; for example, she would say, 'The priest said to I...'

I found out later that this misuse of 'I' is a quirk of a certain West Country dialect, but, in his wisdom, God used it to reveal something to me. I was meditating on Moses' call at the burning bush, and in particular God's answer to Moses' question, 'Who shall I say has sent me?' Imagine walking into parliament or the White House with some instructions—wouldn't the first question be, 'Who are you?' The issue is one of authority that we all face when we set out on a task. 'Who are you?' is the same question as, 'By what authority do you tell me what to do?' Moses knew that he would be asked this by Pharaoh, but more than that, he had his *own* inner doubts and insecurities... *'Who am I?'*

I understood that God's answer, 'Tell them: I am, has sent me to you!' was an answer at the deepest level. God, who is 'I am', is the foundation of all personality and authority. In effect, God was saying to Moses, 'I am that I am and I am giving yourself to you—so you can say I am has sent *me* to you.' I felt it in my own heart as a healing deep in my personality: 'I am has given myself to me.' He is the giver of personality, of authority, of the right to be me myself—he has given me *me*.

As I received this revelation, I felt my inner identity being stamped deep within me as if by a coining die; three-dimensional and not easily erased. Mary Grace's little West Country foible had opened this up to me because she seemed like such a broken person that she didn't even have 'me'—just the less personal 'I' with the corollary question, 'Who am I?'

## THE FATHER AT THE CROSS

The whole Catholic question remained in my thoughts from time to time, however, and one day when I was thinking about the cross—around the time the old drunk man had told me about Jesus on the Cross still standing over the ruin of the church (obviously Catholic)—I had a vision. In the vision I found myself standing at Golgotha watching Jesus dying on the cross. Then, over the whole scene, the face of the Father came into focus: Jesus dying on the cross was happening right inside his face.

I recognised it as the same face I had seen in my earthly father's face that day when I was about seventeen and had seen in his face the words, 'I would die for you three times'. I could also see that it was the same face, so full of love and acceptance, from that day on the tractor that I had seen again on the road while riding my motorcycle in Belgium only a couple of months before. It was both of those images but also much more. It carried, in those hours at Golgotha, a depth of sorrow and pain beyond anything I could imagine or bear. I could not stop myself from weeping for the next three days.

I knew beyond any doubt that the Father's suffering at the cross was as great as and maybe even greater than

Jesus' suffering. '...*God was in Christ reconciling the world to himself...*' the apostle Paul tells us. (II Corinthians 5:19) And from Jesus himself: '...*you will be scattered, every man to his home, and will leave me alone; yet I am not alone for the Father is with me.*' (John 16:32 at the last supper)

At the root of the Catholic darkness—the dark cave with iron bars vision I had seen in Vienna—was a theological error about the Father: that terrible lie that somehow he had rejected Jesus on the cross, rather than the truth that he was in Him, with Him, and loving Him as always. Indeed, the foundational truth of the cross is that the love between the Father and the Son is stronger than all sin and death. Remove this truth, and the cross is no more than a symbol: just another noble martyr dying for a cause.

Psalm 22, which begins, *'My God, my God why have you forsaken me',* and which Jesus quoted on the cross describes something of the feeling going on in the heart of Father, Son and Spirit at that moment as the horrible disintegration and alienation of sin passed through their tender, loving hearts. Reading further in that Psalm, we find that not only sin but the demon spirits that feed on evil, pictured as bulls, lions and dogs, were tearing and wounding the soft, defenceless persons of our God (Father, Son and Spirit) as they opened their loving hearts to sinners deserving death.

By the time we reach verse 24, we find that, indeed, Jesus had not been abandoned, whatever the feelings: '...*and he hid not his face from him, but has heard when he cried to him.'* That beautiful face of the Father, who had himself been dying for the sins of the world from the beginning, was ever before Jesus—even at his darkest hour.

It isn't just the Catholic Church that has suffered under deception about the Father; many others have also fallen to the doctrine that the Father is the cold, angry, distant one, always judging and condemning. When we feel this way, we seek an intermediary: first Jesus, then perhaps Mary, and then, even she is too holy and distant, so we need saints and priests and so on and so on. In the protestant or charismatic scene it can be the same, only, instead of Mary, saints and priests, we seek the next 'great leader' or 'breakthrough strategy' or 'teaching' or 'movement'.

One thing is certain: it is only the Holy Spirit who can lead us into this truth, not just as an academic idea but as a living, dynamic reality. Only in that dynamic can any of us actually stay free from religion. Of course the Holy Spirit uses words, so let him carry these words into your heart. The true Gospel can be summed up: Jesus came to restore our relationship to the Father. The most beautiful words in all the gospels must surely be those words of Jesus: '... *the Father himself loves you...* ' (John 16:27) Through what Jesus did for us we can set aside our fig leaves of religion and step out into the Father's presence; His tender-hearted trusting children once again—in Eden.

There were several tokens of the victory over this stronghold that came in the months that followed, including people from a Catholic religious background joining the New Life congregation and a fruitful connection with renewed Catholics in Cairo—I even met the Archbishop. One strange thing during the most intense time of praying into this religious stronghold came at the Sunday evening service. I shared some revelation about the Father's presence and sorrow at the cross, and a Catholic theologian from Vancouver, Canada—never seen before or since at that meeting—stood up and made some kind of jumbled response to my words. I'm not sure if this was resistance or affirmation—but either way it confirmed I was on the right track. And then there was some encouraging fruit that came thirty years later—from Vienna, where it all started in the first place. I'll touch on that later.

## Epilogue

An event that took place some nine or ten years later might be considered a small appendix to this section so I'll include it here. I was back in Canada by that time and wounded in other areas of my heart because of how everything had gone in subsequent years in London. At that time, I was very discouraged because the expectations had been so high at the period recounted in this book, and little had seemed to come (in the time frame we imagined) in terms of the 'revival' we were all expecting.

In the wisdom of the years, I am quite happy now to leave all the timings in the hands of He who alone is Lord of the harvest. I can also now see that the accomplishments of the early eighties were complete and that, far from ending in failure, we had already accomplished the task God had given us—and I'm not using the royal 'we' here; I mean the Ichthus Fellowship accomplished the main purpose for which God had brought it together.

But it is hard to make the transition from one era to the next and we all make more mistakes than usual at such times. Besides that, Jesus and the apostles clearly warn us that there will be many trials and troubles in this world. Perhaps this epilogue can serve as a reality check against the sort of triumphal idealism that can also be a snare to our faith.

I had known about Francis and Judith MacNutt for some time but had never heard them in person. Francis, a Catholic priest who had come out of the priesthood and married, still ministered within the charismatic Catholic scene and also to the wider church. Judith, who had trained as a psychologist, also had a powerful ministry. They were both coming as main speakers to a conference in Edmonton, Canada, and my wife Sarah and I decided to go.

At the last meeting of the conference, Judith was speaking about unity and healing across the denominations. I can't remember what she said but she carried such a beautiful anointing of love that I was longing for some touch of it in my heart. I was surprised—maybe even shocked—that at the end of the meeting they announced that they were personally going to pray for every delegate at the conference. There were over five hundred people!

All in attendance were lined up in rows so Francis and Judith could 'leapfrog' down the rows, briefly laying hands on each of us and praying. I found myself—still touched from Judith's ministry and feeling such pain in my heart—saying to the Lord under my breath, 'Please let that lady put her hand right here.' I had my hand on my chest where the pain seemed, if not physical, certainly tangible.

As they came to me it turned out to be Francis who prayed for me and Judith prayed for the person next to me and then they both moved along to the next. Suddenly, after moving along a couple of times, Judith paused... and then came back to me, and pressed both of her hands on my chest and prayed for me. Instantly, the most beautiful love and healing flowed over my heart. It was one of the most powerful touches I have ever experienced from the Lord. She had, even in that busy moment, heard the Lord and bothered to come back in answer to my prayer. The loving detail in that spoke volumes in itself.

The whole experience was also an example of a beautiful and distinctively feminine love from God. Sometimes I wonder if Protestants, in their reaction to the inappropriate worship of Mary by Catholics, have 'thrown out the baby with the bath water' and closed their hearts to many of the beautiful feminine colours of God's love. One thing is certain: it will take the whole church—men, women and children from all denominations and streams—to even *begin* to show the whole range of God's love.

## CHAPTER 8
# THE CHURCH OF ENGLAND: BATTLE AT THE GATE

The battle concerning the Church of England was by far the most complex I got involved with during this period. It had several strands of origin which I did not at first recognise as part of the same fight. The warfare regarding the Catholic Church discussed in the last chapter was preparatory but also a step into the Church of England because the root of all religious strongholds is founded in false views and understandings of God our Father. In various ways, too, I had been prepared for this battle for many years.

### THE MARTYRDOM OF DAVID WATSON

David Watson was an Anglican vicar who had become well known while leading a successful church in York; St Michael le Belfrey. He became known for Holy Spirit renewal within the Anglican Church and his evangelistic ministry took him worldwide. He wrote several books on spiritual warfare and released or encouraged creative ministries of music, dance and drama into the national and international scenes—some of which continue to this day. He moved to London in 1982 and had a lasting impact on St Andrews, Chorley Wood and Holy Trinity Brompton, London—both of these later became leading centres of renewal within the Church of England. Part of David's impact on these congregations was indirect, through connecting with John Wimber of Vineyard, and bringing that ministry to London.

I first heard of David Watson when he was dying of cancer in 1984, and I was immediately led by the Spirit into warfare for his healing. Of course many other people, including John Wimber and his famous healing teams, were involved. For my part, I was in the full flow of warfare into World War II issues at this time and also the revelation of the Father at the cross discussed in previous and later chapters. The power of the cross to turn the tide and bring good out of every evil was foremost in my mind at the time. Indeed, so powerfully was this conviction gripping me that I felt as if I was standing on the brink of limitless faith. I piled into prayer and warfare and prophetic action at every level—fully expecting a healing.

After a few days believing a healing would happen, I began to feel troubled. Then I had a dream and woke up knowing it related to David Watson. In the dream, I was standing in woodland watching Joseph Smith, founder of Mormonism, coming down from the mountain where he had supposedly received the Book of Mormon along with his special glasses. As I watched, a redcoat British soldier arose out of the ground, resurrected from the dead, having fallen in that place a century earlier. He leapt into action and pursued Joseph Smith with military purpose.

A few days later, David Watson died and I for one claimed his death as martyrdom for great eternal consequence. I understood from the dream about the redcoat that through this death—this martyrdom—God is able act into the past against the spiritual root of deception within Mormonism, to the ultimate effect that the whole Mormon community will find eternal salvation through the eternal blood of Christ in the eternal Holy Spirit.

Additionally, the first shoots of the current renewal movement within the Church of England began the following year, 1985. This may not of course be down to David Watson's martyrdom alone, but no renewal of consequence takes place without the seeding of martyr blood somewhere in the mix. However, we must always remember that all glory belongs to Jesus and no other martyrdom would 'make the grade' at all, if not for his perfect one on the cross.

## St Paul's Cathedral

One early spring day in 1984, I was praying for a troubled woman in my congregation. She had been badly injured in a motorcycle accident some twenty years before at the age of about eighteen. Her boyfriend, the driver, who was high on drugs at the time, had been killed in the crash. As I was praying for her healing and, warring into the roots of her condition, I had a vision of a part of an old building—a close-up view of the very top bit—which

I did not recognise, but knew was in London somewhere. I also knew that this picture represented the location of the stronghold of a spirit of destruction which I identified with the Assyrian Empire from the Old Testament. This stronghold is a conglomerate of destructive power against body and soul, health and relationships, body physical and body spiritual, 'violence' and 'false religion'. It is the military and religious power that finds its way generation after generation into the heart of human empires and nations.

The following morning, as I was about to leave my room, the Lord said, 'Leave your watch at home today.' So I took off my watch and went out for a walk in Greenwich Park to pray and see what the Lord had in store for the day. As I stood looking over the city of London, I began to think of the Assyrian Empire and its capital Nineveh, which Jonah, the Old Testament prophet, had eventually preached in—after the whale 'incident'. I remembered from the text that the city of Nineveh was three days' journey across and Jonah had gone a day's journey into it. (Ref: Jonah 3:3-4)

My thoughts ran along the lines: 'London is about three days' journey across (walking) and I'm about a half a day's walk into it already so I'll walk another half a day and see where that is' (parallel to Jonah). I set off down the hill in Greenwich Park, past the Cutty Sark and across the Thames by the foot tunnel to the Isle of Dogs. From there I kept walking as near as I could tell and, with the help of road signs, in the general direction of central London. It is highly probable that I didn't take the most efficient route but precision was obviously not the main issue in this case. (Thinking of it now, it is also obvious that Nineveh was nowhere near the size of London and for it to be a three-day journey across must have meant that the journey was a convoluted and complex one through very dense build-up.)

After walking for several hours, but perhaps not yet half a day—remember, my watch had been left at home upon the prompting of the Holy Spirit—I found myself approaching St Paul's Cathedral. My thought was simply, 'I've never been here before; I think I'll have a look inside.'

Prominently placed throughout the interior, alongside the various accoutrements of religion, were the tombs and monuments of the great military leaders of the British Empire. Reading the epitaph of a venerated field marshal, I began to suspect this was the stronghold of the Assyrian: the spirit of destruction; my quarry.

I went up to the whispering gallery and there noticed a sign pointing towards the entry to the 'lantern', on top of the dome. The staircase leading up to the lantern zigzagged through an attic-type area between the inner dome and the outer dome. In that area the actual supporting structure was not a dome at all, but a cone built of brick. As I climbed the staircase, I was almost overwhelmed by the strange sensation of being able to see that hidden cone both physically and spiritually at the same time. On one hand it was thousands of carefully laid bricks; on the other it existed as spiritual substance—no weird faces or any such thing, just spiritual bricks. This was the dwelling place of the Assyrian spirit, the religious spirit, the spirit of destruction that I had come to find. When I got up to the lantern, I got another surprise. Close up, I could see that it was exactly the bit of architecture I had seen in my vision while praying for the lady injured in the motorcycle accident.

Built on the ashes of the great fire of London, this building had become a secret dwelling place of the spirit of destruction. At home within it were the honoured military men of the empire: Assyrians. Even the hidden cone had the proportions of Assyrian cone-shaped bells from the necks of war horses—this I observed from a photo of an ancient Assyrian relief. I remembered the scripture: '*And on that day there shall be inscribed on the bells of the horses, 'Holy to the Lord'.*' (Zechariah 14:20) From that day and for the following seven years I asserted this word in prayer and held it in my heart for the cleansing of St Paul's Cathedral from the Assyrian spirit.

There was another interesting connection with the Assyrian cone shape as well. During my first year working in Greenwich, I had gone to an after-concert party with my violinist friend from the National Centre for Orchestral Studies course. During the evening, I had struck up a conversation with one of the musicians and somehow we got onto all things spiritual. He had a drug problem which he was quite open, but also quite desperate, about. Recently he had had a very 'bad trip' as they used to call it—I can't remember what term he used. He said a 'large upside-down cone' had appeared to him and demanded that he bow before it. (By the way, I have never figured out which way a cone would be considered 'upside-down'—but that's what he said.) At first, I just thought it was one of those 'weird things you hear at parties'; but on reflection, I realised it was some kind of demonic encounter... which is probably what 'bad trips' always have been.

After the St Paul's experience of perceiving the spiritual element in the cone motif, I saw the obvious connection with drugs (the original motorcycle accident had involved drugs), and the Assyrian spirit of destruction. And of course the old imperial spirit has a long complicity in the worldwide drugs trade. I remembered reading about revivals in some imperial Asian outpost a hundred years earlier, when children had seen visions of certain demons that were under no pressure to leave—even with the revival going on—because those in authority had turned a blind eye, or even aided the drugs trade. (The Opium wars of the mid nineteenth had been fought by the British, *not against the opium trade, but to keep it going!*)

A second element in the battle with the Assyrian spirit came through this scripture: *'And this shall be peace, when the Assyrian comes into our land and treads upon our soil that I will raise up against him seven shepherds and eight princes of men; they shall rule the land of Assyria with the sword; and the land of Nimrod with the drawn sword; and they shall deliver us from the Assyrian when he comes into our land and treads within our border.'* (Micah 5:5-6)

The shepherds are pastors, and the princes of men I took to be apostles. These are the gifts and authorities that must be raised up to overcome the Assyrian. Within the poetic and prophetic symmetry of the Old Testament, the shepherd became king (David); in the New Testament, pastors become apostles (Peter). Apostles are those 'sent' (meaning of apostle) by the Father, just as Jesus had been sent. Ultimate authority—deep, true Godly love—is grown into by feeding and tending the sheep, just as Peter had been instructed in John 21:15ff. The way, therefore, to battle this stronghold is to care for the sheep such as praying for healing—after all, this journey started with praying for a woman injured in a motorcycle accident involving drugs. And of course direct aggressive spiritual warfare is involved in true pastoral care. Notice the phrases: *'with the sword'* and *'with the drawn sword.'*

A third element in the warfare to cleanse St Paul's was important as far as my personal involvement was concerned. In looking into the history, I discovered that the building had been financed by a 'coal tax'—a tax on coal brought into London. I immediately knew in my spirit that, far from being an innocuous bit of bureaucracy, this had literally translated into people being cold—especially the poorest children—because of the extra cost of heating. My own underlying call for this season of intercession was based on the revelation of the Father's heart for people who were cold. The experience of seeing the Father's face when my hands were cold on the motorcycle trip across Belgium had given me access to the Father's heart and authority in this area, and the knowledge and revelation about St Paul's (the coal tax in this case) was my access to the stronghold on earth.

*The Gates of Eden*

The mandate was to bring judgement against the Assyrian religious and political stronghold that had been empowered through the coal tax. The fact that three centuries had passed has no relevance in the eternal councils of heaven, and an unrelenting weight of judgement was levied by God the Father, against this spirit, for the next seven years. But of course I only had my hands on the pipes of God's great hydraulic system; the pressure inside those pipes was far beyond what any human soul could have borne.

## KING HENRY'S LEGACY

One way that discernment operates is entirely non-mystical; rather, it follows plain logic and is therefore immune from some of the complex deceptions by which Satan has sought to shroud himself within religion. The religious spirit is a particularly slippery operator and some plain facts are a great antidote to its confusing emotional overtures.

We have already been discussing the concoction of military and religion that I have been calling the 'Assyrian' or the 'spirit of destruction'. This stronghold within the Church of England, besides the macro imperial and war element, had various expressions including accidents and illness. Another expression was the breakdown of marriages—and relationships in general for that matter. The roots of this stronghold precede the building of St Paul's, going back to the actual founding of the Church of England

The logic regarding the destructive pressure against marriage comes into play like this: Henry VIII is the founder of the Church of England, against the background of and to facilitate his murderous and destructive behaviour towards his wives. This destructive seed remains in the foundation of the Church until it is removed. This truth, by definition, supersedes any emotional and mystical cloaking of the truth—parallel to the way the cone concealed between two domes in St Paul's remains nevertheless the actual reality that holds up the whole roof.

Once again, with the pastor heart revelation from Micah quoted in the last section, I launched an assault against the Assyrian from this angle as well. The battle was fought in the heart of my own congregation—our lives together given over to God to be a stone in his sling against the Assyrian 'Goliath'. The battle raged on over several years—many nights and days of prayer, fasting and aggressive spiritual warfare were required to maintain a constant flow of love in the Holy Spirit.

A token of the coming breakthrough came with the first wedding in my newly planted congregation. A man who had encouraged me to come to Greenwich in the first place got married to a Church of England vicar's daughter, a student nurse who had joined us earlier that year. (By the way, this is the man who owned number 7 Combedale Road, the house mentioned in an earlier chapter, where we had seen victory over both occult and religious spirits.) The wedding was in Hampshire at her father's church but they invited me to be the preacher. Three Anglican bishops and several vicars were in attendance. The event felt strangely prophetic and completely beyond my youthful experience—but I waded in with my best shot.

Several of the elderly bishops spoke kindly to me afterward with helpful advice, so I knew my preaching was poor enough to elicit their sympathy; but I also knew God was at work in spite of my weakness. In that first wedding, the gauntlet was dropped and the fight was on. Several years later, we came to a year of breakthrough and had twelve marriages in the congregation—including my own.

The insights from the final chapter, 'Travailing Desire', came during this period of battle against the roots of destruction against marriage in the Henry VIII stronghold. (I've put most of that material at the end because it also has a wider application to intercession generally and to the church as bride of Christ.) Beside the aggressive 'drawn swords' fighting with the 'word' of God, there must always be an intercessory side, an inner face of the battle. Jeremiah touches this inner heart element: *'For the wound of the daughter of my people is my heart wounded, I mourn and dismay has taken hold of me. Is there no balm in Gilead? Is there no physician there? Why then has the health of the daughter of my people not been restored?* (Jeremiah 8:21-22)

The addition of intercession, aggressive spiritual warfare, and prophetic action at all levels, brings change to the whole historical matrix. It follows logically that the total sum of the history has changed. Henry's actual historic actions remain of course but now there is another factor—an addition to the total history which changes the spiritual dwelling place in the present. Every prophetic addition to the total history of the Church of England—or, rather, I should say, to the whole church in England—made it a less comfortable home for the religious 'Assyrian' spirit. At some tipping point, that spirit is cast out—root and branch—by the Holy Spirit.

## Queen Elizabeth's Oak

Greenwich Park, besides being near my congregation, had been the royal residence in the days of King Henry VIII. His daughter and heir, Queen Elizabeth I, had played in the park (palace gardens at that time) as a child and an ancient oak tree had been named 'Queen Elizabeth's Oak' because she had apparently had a tea party in its great hollow truck. This tree, a seedling in the twelfth century—so already over four hundred years old in Henry's day—had died sometime near the end of the nineteenth century but its hollow, ivy-covered trunk still stood in 1984.

One day I was praying in the park and as I walked past the tree, I asked God to mark the day of complete breakthrough on the Henry VIII stronghold in the Church of England by having this tree fall down. I immediately knew this was a Holy Spirit-inspired request and that God responded with a clear 'yes'. The tree became an indicator in the battle.

All through the subsequent months, I often walked past the tree to gauge my progress in the battle. Month after month, year after year, the tree stood firm. In 1987, a severe wind storm swept across the south of England and I rushed down to the park next morning—almost certain the tree would be down. What? Still standing?

Hundreds of healthy trees had come down on the streets and in the park but this ancient one, dead a hundred years, was still standing. I wondered if it would ever fall—the storm had been the worst in a century. Of course there would be no benefit in knocking the tree down myself (the thought did cross my mind). That would be like bending the fuel gauge needle on a car and expecting fuel to be added to the tank. The tree was only an indicator; a very helpful tool in prayer and spiritual warfare if used properly, and utter nonsense if not.

I continued my prayer and held my ground until one day in 1991 the tree fell. Not a great wind storm, but a persistent soaking rain had finally brought it down. The season was complete; the job was done, and I rested it all with the Lord.

A beginning of change began that very year in the Church of England—though most changes weren't seen till later. I noted one at the time. George Carey, an outsider, but proper born-again Christian, was appointed Archbishop of Canterbury (highest office in the Church of England). I say *outsider* because the church council puts forward two names to the prime minister; one is expected to be chosen and the other is just a token to 'pretend' the prime minister actually has a choice. Margaret Thatcher, prime minister at the time, defied tradition and chose the outsider and unexpected George Carey. And I said, 'Hallelujah!'

## First Fruits

From 1991, many changes began to take place within the Church of England. Holy Trinity Brompton and St Andrews Chorley Wood, both influenced significantly by David Watson, became two of the main centres of renewal within the whole Church. One of the most significant things, with hindsight to 1991, is that Nicky Gumble took leadership of the Alpha Course that year. The Alpha Course had been HTB's local discipleship programme, but from 1991 it exploded into the international phenomena it is today. Nicky had been powerfully impacted and called out of a career as barrister through the ministry of John Wimber back in 1984—the same year David Watson died.

Also through John Wimber's ministry in London in 1984, an oil industry executive named Justin Welby found salvation and a new ministry calling. Some twenty-nine years later (2013) he was anointed Archbishop of Canterbury—the first fruits of the current renewal to reach that place of authority in the Church of England. And to complete the lovely prophetic symmetry, for the first time in history, a woman performed the actual anointing of the Archbishop. That woman was none other than Anne Watson, the widow of David Watson.

And of special interest to me, at a large conference hosted by HTB later that same year, a special guest, the Catholic Archbishop of Vienna—a godly, proper Christian—was an invited speaker. David Watson had always had a heart to build bridges with the Catholics but for me the significance went beyond that. My whole journey of warfare against religious strongholds had begun with a vision in a Catholic Church in Vienna in 1981 and reached completion with the fall of Queen Elizabeth's Oak in 1991. That God had brought renewal to Catholics in Vienna and Anglicans in England was a cause for joy in answered prayer. Of course I know that many people shared that battle over many years and some put in much more effort and paid a much higher price than I did, but it's still fun to have a part in the 'big picture' things God does.

As for King Henry's legacy and St Paul's Cathedral, consider these amazing things. Presiding at St Paul's now, the current Bishop of London, Richard Chartres, is that lovely man of God who preached to the whole world at the wedding of William and Catherine, Duke and Duchess of Cambridge (future king and queen). And that beautiful wedding (at Westminster Abbey, and done jointly with Catholics) released joy and healing into the heart of a nation wounded by the tragic failure of the previous royal marriage—from before the renewal. Not only that, but similar to the Alpha course, the HTB Marriage Course has become a worldwide blessing to marriages both in the church and beyond it (40 languages in 109 countries and growing—according to an article in The Guardian, 28/12/2013). What a beautiful, gentle and loving Saviour Jesus and Father God we serve in the Holy Spirit!

## CHAPTER 9
# LORD OF THE WHOLE EARTH: GATE OF THE PEOPLES

### DIALECTIC

When I lived in the house on Beaconsfield Road, I discovered a spiritual principle: what I did in the Holy Spirit—including all the normal domestic chores—had a direct connection to the atmosphere in the whole house. This was why my neighbour, who was demonised, reacted against it in her 'opposing spirit', and wrecked her room, when I had cleaned and repaired mine.

Many people involved in spiritual warfare have applied this principle, to a mission situation for example, by acting in an 'opposite spirit' to the prevailing spirit of a particular territory, area, city or country. Say you were working in an area where people were very stingy; the best strategy to overcome it is to be very generous. This is an essential element of all kingdom work—we must always live in a Godly and righteous way and not give in to the prevailing unrighteousness. If we just 'go with the flow', we will not be fruitful or effective; we will just expand the problem, and not provide a solution.

This seemingly sophisticated spiritual warfare principle is in fact the most basic Christianity. It is found in two of Jesus' most frequently quoted teachings: 'Do to others as you would have them do to you' and, 'Turn the other cheek.' (Ref: Matthew 7:12; 5:39) And it is the heart of the cross; overcoming evil and hatred, with goodness and love. This must be the central principle in our lives, both as individuals and corporately, as true Church.

In the last section I mentioned spiritual warfare where the church is pitted against an evil stronghold on earth. The Holy Spirit led me to hold my congregation as a lamp in a dark place; as light in darkness, in the battle to purify the Church of England from the 'Assyrian' stronghold of destruction. Put another way, this is quite simply to live out as a congregation the reality of what you are praying. Of course this must be in the Holy Spirit, and the various levels of spiritual access in this case were managed by the Holy Spirit—it was well over my head; I only had my hands on 'dad's hydraulic system'.

This kind of spiritual warfare could be called prophetic action in one way of thinking or, more formally, the assertion of an ideal using a complex set of universals. Either way, it is truth asserted against error or light shining into darkness; a righteous society pressing a standard into an unrighteous society; love neutralising 'unlove'. Israel was supposed to be that light to the nations of the earth in its day; the church is meant to be a city set on a hill and a light to the nations in our day. Jesus said, 'You are the light of the world.' (Matthew 5:14) And the apostle Paul said '...*that through the church the manifold wisdom of God might now be made know to the principalities and powers in the heavenly places.'* (Ephesians 3:10)

Whatever society or solidarity God builds for his own habitation on earth—tabernacle, temple, nation or church—the result will be that the light of his heart and mind and actions will shine into the whole earth. The thoughts of the Father's great heart are truly the light of the world. They were perfectly expressed by Jesus in first-century Palestine. Since Jesus' ascension to heaven, this light shines through his body—i.e., the church filled with the Holy Spirit—throughout the whole earth. God's lordship over the earth had been lost with Adam and Eve but in Christ, and through his body the church, it is being fully restored.

We will look at the nature of this conflict, which I am going to call 'dialectic'; a term with origins among the Greek philosophers but perhaps most famously applied to history by the German philosopher Hegel—the 'Hegelian Dialectic'. 'Dialectic' means 'argument' and in this context we are talking about the 'argument' going on in the cosmos between the light of God's heart and the dark mind of the serpent.

It is quite wrong to view this battle in dualistic terms as if two opponents faced each other in a neutral arena. There is no such arena, and the darkness cannot fight the light; it can only block by lies, confusion, and strongholds of deception, which blind all who believe the serpent. Dispelling those lies and breaking those strongholds is the Church's battle. This is not so much a question of what the church says or prays as what the church actually is—a society of those living the reality of God's love. This love of God lived out in reality in the Holy Spirit is the light that will overcome in the dialectic with the world.

## JERUSALEM: GATE OF THE PEOPLES

*'Son of man, because Tyre has said concerning Jerusalem, 'Aha, the gate of the peoples is broken, it has swung open to me; I shall be replenished, now that she is laid waste,' therefore thus says the Lord God: Behold I am against you oh Tyre, and will bring up many nations against you, as the sea brings up its waves.'*
(Ezekiel 26:2-4)

In the Old Testament period, Jerusalem was called by God to be the righteous city that pressed its righteousness onto the cities of the world. In the verse quoted, Jerusalem is called 'the gate of the peoples' because it was God's gate (his authority) that was being exerted through Jerusalem out to the people of the whole earth. When Jerusalem fell into unrighteousness and the subsequent judgement of exile in Babylon, Tyre feels that the restraints and limitations are gone—the gate is broken, it has swung open—Tyre can do what she wants again. And since Tyre was the financial stronghold, that meant getting rich and powerful again.

It is interesting to note the many other events in the world during Jerusalem's demise. Clearly it was not just Tyre who felt the restraints were off. Indeed, the cat was away and now the mice could play! Secular historians, without the reference to Jerusalem I'm making here, still refer to this period of history as an 'axial period'. 'Axial Period' is generally understood to mean a major change in human thinking or consciousness.

In the period of Jerusalem's Babylonian exile, several of the so-called 'great world religions' arose. These include Buddhism (which branched off from ancient Hinduism); Hinduism (in its current form); Zoroastrianism (dualistic religion of the Persians); and the kind of Greek thinking which informs the basic Western mindset. Of course we don't think of our 'Western mindset' as a 'religion'; but in fact it actually is religion too, at least in the sense that it engages the same part of the human spirit that religion does. It doesn't really matter whether we call it religion or philosophy of course—either way we are speaking of a change in mindset or consciousness.

The connection I'm making is that this axial change in corporate consciousness occurred during the time of Jerusalem's exile because the restraint against false religion, deceptive philosophy, and financial exploitation that a righteous Jerusalem *would* have provided was curtailed during this period. The front line of the cosmic battle had been pushed back, in favour of error and deception.

When the people of God stand in righteousness, now as then, the battle line will move the other way in favour of truth, righteous trade, freedom and goodness. The Proverbs capture the idea like this: *'When justice is done it is a joy to the righteous, but dismay to evil doers.'* (21:15) And again: *'Those who forsake the law praise the wicked, but those who keep the law strive against them.'* (28:4)

## LORD OF ALL THE EARTH

*'And the angel answered me, "These are going forth to the four winds of heaven, after presenting themselves before the Lord of all the earth. The chariot with the black horses goes toward the north country, the white ones go toward the west country, and the dappled ones go toward the south country." When the steeds came out they were impatient to get off and patrol the earth. And he said, "Go patrol the earth." So they patrolled the earth.'*
(Zechariah 6: 5-7)

The picture of chariots patrolling the earth from this Zechariah passage reinforces and enlarges our understanding of how the righteous city, Jerusalem, exerted God's authority into the world. Parallel to the city of Jerusalem (including the temple) being rebuilt, the authority of God into the world, through it, is being restored. The restraints against evil are back in position; the gate has swung shut again—the cat is back; beware, mice.

Appropriately the reference to God is 'Lord of all the

earth'. This term is first used when Joshua led the people across the Jordan and into the Promised Land. Hence the possessing of the land of Israel was the first step in the programme of God ruling not just that bit of earth but literally the whole earth. After the interrupting exile in Babylon, Jerusalem is rebuilt and the programme is back on track.

Jerusalem has become God's 'base' or 'beach head' again and from it 'chariots' are sent out to patrol the earth. This is a picture of God's authority being exerted out from Jerusalem to restrain evil and exert the goodness, beauty and truth of heaven. 'Chariots' speak of the prophetic ministry as we first see when Elisha received Elijah's mantle of ministry. (Ref: II Kings 2:12) The prophetic ministry was Israel's chariots and horsemen; they were not to have literal chariots and horsemen like the Egyptians and other worldly nations. When Israel held faith and honoured her prophets instead of killing them, the word of the Lord went out from Jerusalem and light shone to all the nations around them.

Even when Jerusalem was not very righteous, it still exerted some of God's authority. It is worth noting that from the days of David and Solomon (about 1000 BC) to the time of Jesus, it was only during the seventy years of Babylonian exile that God did not have authority to some degree in Jerusalem. And in that period he still had outstanding prophets like Ezekiel and Daniel—in exile themselves—through whom he maintained some authority on earth. (Of course, God is also able to use non-believers or other nations to get some things done, but this is never his first or preferred choice.)

The 'prophetic beach head in exile' (Ezekiel, Daniel and others) still accomplished a great deal and Daniel's prophetic intercessions shone light, not only in Babylon and Persia, but forward to the coming of Christ and beyond. No doubt Daniel meditated on such words as, *'And nations shall come to your light, and kings to the brightness of your rising.'* (Isaiah 60:3) He fulfilled these words in his own context as adviser and prophet to Nebuchadnezzar, Belshazzar and Darius; and God's people in every era—whether outwardly appearing strong or weak—have the same privilege and mandate. God's purpose is always to take over the whole earth, for in truth he is 'Lord of all the Earth', and he will persevere *'...for nothing can hinder the Lord from saving by many or by few.'* (I Samuel 14:6b)

For an application of the 'patrolling chariots' mentioned in the Zechariah passage quoted above, I will make a connection with my prayer involving the ship and the six drive belts. Zechariah also prophesied about the four smiths who were sent to cast down the four horns of the nations that had scattered Judah. (Ref: Zechariah 1:20-21) The chariots are 'machines' built by 'smiths' to exert God's authority—a kind of prayer. This, like my use of the ship and drive belts, is complex prophetic prayer; the use of multiple complex universals to assert 'words' in the spiritual realm. By the use of this kind of 'spiritual machinery', we can say much more than a few sentences could carry. The learning, knowledge and skill of

*The Gates of Eden*

years can be asserted in a single moment by this method. It is in this way that we 'hammer our ploughshares into swords'. We use the skills, trades, professions, and crafts that we have in this world to create 'machines' or 'mechanisms' or 'devices' or 'setups' in our minds in the Spirit (prayer) that convey God's truth and authority. Every skill and knowledge that we have in the natural realm can be transposed into the spiritual realm for kingdom purposes. In this paradigm, the intricacies, detail and authority of many 'ploughshares' can, in the Holy Spirit, be converted into spiritual 'swords'. *'Beat your ploughshares into swords, and your pruning hooks into spears; let the weak say, "I am a warrior."'* (Joel 3:10)

This level of prophetic praying is a two-edged sword. On the one hand we can use every natural skill in spiritual warfare, but on the other we can also connect every natural activity into the spirit, even while we are doing it. An ordinary working day in any profession can be transposed in the Holy Spirit into spiritual salt and light for use by the Lord of the Whole earth, wherever he chooses to apply it. On both edges of this 'sword', the labour and skill of a lifetime can be exerted in moments; and the equivalent to thousands of hours of prayer can be released in a day. But don't try to set it up outside of the Holy Spirit—only in Jesus can such weight be carried.

*Vance Royal Olson*

# THE CHURCH: LIGHT OF THE WORLD, SALT OF THE EARTH

*'You are the salt of the earth; but if salt has lost its taste, how shall its saltiness be restored? It is no longer good for anything except to be thrown out and trodden under foot by men. You are the light of the world. A city set on a hill cannot be hid. Nor do men light a lamp and put it under a bushel basket, but on a stand, and it gives light to all in the house. Let your light so shine before men, that they may see your good works and give glory to your Father who is in heaven.'*
(Matthew 5: 13-16)

I know that some people would raise an eyebrow when, in the last chapter, I said I pitted my congregation against the Assyrian stronghold, like the stone in David's sling against Goliath. Should a pastor not protect his flock, hide it in God and avoid spiritual conflicts as much as possible? Many fear spiritual backlash and therefore shrink from all spiritual warfare. I guess they would like to take their lamp to some place that is already so bright that its light will not be noticed, or hide it so well it can never seen. Surely, this has never been God's way.

The teaching and tenor of scripture points us in the opposite direction. Consider the verse above: light of the world, city on a hill, lamp on a stand, let your light so shine and so on. Of course persecution and pressure will come against those who seek to live righteously. Jesus said: *'Blessed are those who are persecuted for righteousness' sake, for theirs is the kingdom of heaven.'* (Matthew 5:10) And the apostle Paul said: *'Indeed all who desire to live a godly life in Christ Jesus will be persecuted ...'* (2 Timothy 3:12) Just by living a righteous life in this world, we are a threat to the incumbent authority, our very lives asserting God's authority.

The answer to persecution or threat or danger must be to keep on shining even more light, not to hide. As I read Jesus' words here, he is saying that, far from being something to avoid, enduring pressure is in fact key to inheriting the kingdom of heaven. This is also affirmed by *'...through many tribulations* (literally: 'pressures') *we must enter the kingdom of God.'* (Acts 14:22)

A life, and especially our lives jointly, lived righteously against the grain of an unrighteous world, asserts God's will, his light into darkness. This is not a special branch of church work; it is the central reason for the church and the unavoidable reality of living righteously, as we are called to. The great thing about it is we are promised success: *'Let your light so shine before men, that they may see your good works and give glory to your Father who is in Heaven.'* (Matthew 5:16)

## A Surprising Observation

Sometimes the church is criticised, even by its own leaders and members, for not being much more outstandingly righteous than the world around it. Additionally, critics note that some non-Christians seem to live just as righteously as many Christians. Should we find this discouraging? No, we should not! Rather, the reverse.

What people who speak this way fail to understand is how the world and these righteous individuals would get on if the righteous influence of Godly people and the church was removed from the equation. The Babylonian exile of Jerusalem provides a partial historic example, but even then the prophets plugged the gap. What would happen if this 'dialectic' was fully disengaged? We would have to assume it would be worse than the days of Noah; for even then, Noah, Methuselah and others still stood in righteousness. And we would have to assume it would be worse than Sodom and Gomorrah; for in those cities, the righteous soul of Lot was vexed by the evil around him. (Ref: 2 Peter 2:7-8)

The upshot of the teaching in this chapter is that a restraint against evil and a positive righteous influence is exerted by God's people over the whole earth. We should not therefore lament, 'Oh, the church is no better than the world;' rather, we should rejoice: 'Wow, the world is as righteous as the church: the salt is working!' Of course I'm not saying we shouldn't improve by being saltier and brighter. But we should recognise that, as we become more righteous, we will be 'towing the whole world up the hill' with us. From this we can infer two things about being righteous: one, it will be more difficult than we expect; and two, it is far more important and worthwhile than we imagine. Every truly righteous deed is world-changing. The story of Esther, Mordecai and Haman (from the biblical book, Esther) illustrates this principle beautifully. One righteous man, Mordecai, prevented the evil Haman from having his wicked way, even though everyone else was bowing to him.

Throughout history the true Church has been salt and light to the world, and even now bears a far greater load than is generally believed. Ultimately, with Christ, the Church will rule over the whole earth. Of course, that load is unbearable unless we connect ourselves first to Jesus and the easy yoke of his righteousness. Apart from staying connected with Jesus, we are certain to fall as Jerusalem did; losing our saltiness, becoming useless and fit only to be trodden underfoot. (Ref: Matthew 5:13) For the connected and 'abiding', however, Jesus' words apply: *'I have said this to you, that <u>in me</u> you may have peace. In the world you will have tribulations (pressures), but be of good cheer, I have overcome the world.'* (John 16:33)

One thing I should make clear: in talking about ruling the world, I don't mean seeking worldly power such as the church has sometimes done. I'm talking about spiritual ruling in the Holy Spirit. Those who rule with Christ in this way do not require positions within the realms of worldly power—military, religious, political or financial. If we do gain positions in the world they must be secondary and submitted to God (as in Daniel's case, for example) or we will end up crossing over to the other side: resisting the righteous, and promoting the unrighteous (e.g., Balaam, Ref: Numbers 22:5ff). This was the position of the ruling Sanhedrin of Jesus' day. Jerusalem, under their authority, had become in truth a 'Jericho' opposing the purposes of God. Thankfully, the heavenly actions of one righteous man, Jesus, prevailed; the rule of God was secured, and the cross triumphed over all the rulers of the fallen world.

> *'He disarmed the principalities and powers and made a public example of them, triumphing over them in him.'*
> (Colossians 2:15)

## CHAPTER 10
# TRAVAILING DESIRE: ENTERING THE GATES

*'...a desire fulfilled is a tree of life.'*
(Proverbs 13:12)

### *The Day is Done*

*When day is done, and the darkness*
*Falls from the wings of night,*
*As a feather is wafted downward*
*From an eagle in his flight.*

*I see the lights of the village*
*Gleam through the rain and the mist,*
*And a feeling of sadness comes o'er me,*
*That my soul cannot resist:*

*A feeling of sadness and longing,*
*That is not akin to pain,*
*And resembles sorrow only*
*As the mist resembles the rain.*
(Opening stanzas from *The Day is Done* by Henry Wadsworth Longfellow)

The feeling, here identified by Longfellow, is universal to the human experience. Who has not paused for deeper-than-normal thought at that moment when the cut and thrust of the day begins to subside and the deep places of the heart emerge for attention? In the Garden of Eden, God came to Adam and Eve in the evening, to walk with them among the trees; to chat over the day's work; perhaps to find out all the names they were choosing—but mostly just to enjoy the pleasure of the evening ambience with His son and daughter, His friends.

We have longed for that level of closeness to our creator ever since and it seems to be at that same time of the day, twilight, that the deep memory of our ancient ancestors awakens in our human consciousness and we feel—maybe even know—that we are destined for something greater. The sadness and longing, though sorrowful, teeter on the very edge of joy. There is a sense that, if we could but focus just right, we might see what we long to see; or if we could just quiet our mind enough, we might hear that voice we long to hear. And then it slips away just as we become conscious that we are thinking it.

When we are restored in our relationship with our heavenly Father, through the death and resurrection of Jesus and by the direct conscious access that the Holy Spirit conveys to us, we will find ourselves growing deeper and deeper in the satisfaction and fulfilment of this deep longing. Even as we grow deeper in fulfilment, however, we will also begin to sense an even deeper sorrow. We find ourselves on a journey into the sorrow that was there in the Father's heart that day when he called out for Adam and Eve and they were hiding from him.

The loss and pain in the Father's heart, on the tragic evening in Eden, are far greater than any human heart could bear. Even though we are in the gospel age, when the great work of the cross is already accomplished, there are many who are still lost; estranged from their Father like lost sheep on a stormy hillside. It is for these that the Father's heart still aches and it is for these that we are invited into a deep fellowship of sorrow and resolution. This is the inner face of intercession.

More than just prayer, however, this intercession overflows into evangelism and discipleship and even beyond that into a life integrated with the Father's desire and purpose. There is never 'just words' with Him. His words and actions are one, and in the same way, when we walk in this fellowship with him, all the aspects of our lives will integrate and flow together in unity.

The life of Abraham and Sarah is an example of this. Father desired to bring a son to birth, having already promised Adam and Eve that salvation would come through him, and that through him, the serpent's head would be crushed. (Genesis 3:15) Abraham and Sarah walked in travailing faith with the Father in bringing this promise to pass. Abraham walked prophetically and before time with the Father to Mt Moriah and experienced the deep sorrow of giving a son over to death, and through to the joy of resurrection.

Many of the strange actions of the prophets arose out of this fellowship of sorrow or intercession with the Father. Jacob is another example. He lived for many years believing Joseph was dead before receiving him back by resurrection as it were. He then very strangely claimed Joseph's two sons, Ephraim and Manasseh, as his own, giving the reason: *'Rachael to my sorrow died... on the way to Bethlehem.'* (Genesis 48:7) God the Father was on the way to Bethlehem and Jacob walked the sorrowful road with him during his generation.

The relationship of Jacob and Rachael was itself a prophetic intercession. Firstly Jacob had to work seven years for Rachael and even after that he was tricked by her father Laban and ended up with the less desirable sister Leah. Secondly, I infer from Jacob's claiming of Joseph's two sons, that Jacob and Rachael had had a dream of having four sons together, which had subsequently miscarried so horribly with Rachael's death and Joseph being sold into slavery by his older brothers (sons of Jacob by Leah). Near the end of his life, Jacob received his son Joseph back, along with the two grandsons whom he blessed as his own. The writer of Chronicles notes that the birthright (the one stolen from Esau) actually went to the sons of Joseph—that is, Ephraim, whom Jacob had blessed with his right hand even though he was the younger. (Ref: I Chronicles 5:1-2) That birthright is the birthright of the overcomer; of the one who wrestles with God and prevails; the one who, like Abraham and Sarah, perseveres in faith. This, in our times, is the birthright of all Christians—though not all will choose to receive it.

By walking in faith through seeming total failure, Jacob became the father of those who overcome against impossible odds. Through his own heart, joined to the Father in fellowship and wrestling, came the cry across the generations that echoed all the way to Bethlehem: *'A voice is heard in Ramah, wailing and loud lamentation, Rachael weeping for her children, she refuses to be comforted because they are no more.'* (Matthew 2:18) This heart-wrenching cry was forged in Jacob's heart during the hard years of apparent failure when he believed Joseph was dead.

Samuel's mother, Hannah, who was literally from Ramah and an Ephraimite and therefore a daughter (generations later) of Jacob and Rachael, no doubt felt the pang of that same cry as she gave little Samuel to service in the tabernacle. It was the recurring cry across generations of failure and loss. And finally there at Bethlehem when the saviour was born, Matthew applies the words (first actually penned by Jeremiah—31:15) to the babies slaughtered by Herod. Herod is a type of Satan who angrily and vengefully destroys innocent children in resistance of God's purposes. This same 'fingerprint' of Satan can be seen when Pharaoh ordered the male newborn of the Hebrews to be killed and baby Moses escaped in his little reed basket.

Many prophetic people agree that it is the same motivation—the wish to thwart God's deliverers—that lies behind the millions of babies slaughtered through abortion in our times. The devil knows that his time is short and, being a murderer from the beginning, he rages to hurt and destroy as much as possible. He rages against the generation of the 'overcomers' of Revelation; of the end time's apostles, sent in the Father's heart, who will witness the final victory and the great harvest at the end of the age.

Joshua, who led Israel into the Promised Land, is a type of Christ not only because his name is the same as Jesus (the Hebrew form), but because he is from the tribe of Ephraim and therefore an overcomer in the flow of Jacob and Rachael as well. By heritage and birthright he typifies those apostles of the last age who will lead the Church into the Kingdom age—the Promised Land—when Christ reigns on earth. These overcomers are the spiritual sons and daughters of Jacob and Rachael; of Joseph, Ephraim, Joshua, Hannah and Samuel; of those who travail and overcome in the desires and sorrows and joys of the Father's great heart.

We might also develop the idea from the quote above that it is the feminine, mother dimension of God's heart that is particularly in view because it is Rachael who is specifically named and Hannah who is implied by the Ramah reference. Then again, it was Jacob who first experienced weeping over Rachael's 'lost children'—Joseph; Rachael's first born. In this we see that in God is both mother and father heart. Man and woman together were created in His image. The entire prophetic matrix I've been discussing provides a window into the masculine and feminine heart of God, who is at once the pragmatist taking action, and the weeping heart not comforted. True ministry, to which all Christians are called, must combine this reality through the outer face of service and proclamation, and the inner face of intercession.

We see this perfectly and succinctly revealed by Jesus at the tomb of Lazarus as he weeps over the death (intercession) and then raises the dead (action). (Ref: John 11:35, 43) Our age is the crescendo of the ages, all of which have to some extent borne the same paradox of joy and mingled sorrow. In the great shakings and troubles that have come and are coming upon the earth, of which Jesus has warned us, let us find this same stride Jesus had. If we rush off as 'triumphalists', we will fall to pride, but if we only mope in sorrows, we will fall to self pity. Rather let us walk with him in sorrowing and rejoicing; in sowing and in reaping; in prayer and proclamation. We are told in Psalm 126:6 that: *'He that goes forth weeping, bearing the seed for sowing, shall come home with shouts of joy, bringing his sheaves with him.'*

This verse speaks of something deep and beautiful that we are invited to share with our heavenly Father, in fellowship with Jesus, and all the great men and women of faith throughout history. That majestic company will ultimately celebrate a feast beneath the trees of Eden, in a twilight filled with unspeakable joy. There in lamp-lit ambience, at the axis of the ages and the turning of the times, they will savour the glorious foods of the nations and drink wines from the ancient cellars of Heaven. One moment at that table is—and shall be deemed by all to be—beautiful and precious; literally priceless and beyond the reach of all worldly wealth and power. Therefore Jesus counselled: *'Go sell your possessions and give to the poor, and you will have treasures in Heaven ...'* (Matthew 19:21)

Then of course the great feast, which is also called the marriage feast of the lamb, brings another facet of Jacob and Rachael's travail into view. Whereas God was in travail to bring forth a son in the Old Testament period, now in the church age the travail has been to bring forth a bride for that son. Jacob participated in both; seven years for Leah, who bore Judah, through whom the Messiah was born; and then another seven years for Rachael, who bore Joseph, the archetypal overcomer. The life of Jacob and Rachael prophetically foreshadows Jesus' travail of love for his bride—the true church—and shines a light toward the ultimate consummation of masculinity and femininity. Therefore the Bible finishes its story, in reference to Jesus, with these words: *'The Spirit and bride say, 'Come.' And let him who hears say, 'Come.' And let him who is thirsty come, let him who desires take the waters of life without price.'* (Revelation 22:17)

## Appendix 1

# The Reality of Universals

*'Universal: A term or concept of general application. A nature or essence signified by a general term.'*
Oxford Concise Dictionary

*'Universal: A general concept or term, or something in reality to which it corresponds: essence.'*
Merriam-Webster Dictionary

*'In metaphysics, a universal is what particular things have in common, namely characteristics or qualities. In other words, universals are repeatable or recurrent entities that can be instantiated or exemplified by many particular things.'*
Wikipedia

I've added this appendix because it digs into John Wycliffe's philosophy a bit more deeply. Some of the ideas have already been delineated in a less philosophical way in the sections about knowledge and spiritual dwelling places. If you liked those discussions on knowledge, and want more, then you might enjoy this; otherwise I recommend you skip over it. In any case it is only loosely tied to Wycliffe's thought, and represents my own understanding as it has developed over the years. I will pick up the story just after I got the English version of the old Latin book: *Tractatus de Universalibus*.

## REALITY VS. NOMINALISM

My quest to understand and apply Wycliffe's philosophy, encouraged but by no means fully satisfied by the new translation of his book, *On Universals*, led to the wider debate that Wycliffe was participating in. This debate concerned the 'reality' (or otherwise) of universals.

The gauntlet on the reality question had been thrown down, perhaps almost inadvertently, by Porphyry circa 269AD, when, in his introduction to Aristotle's categories, he mused whether universals were 'real' or not, and if real, what the nature of that reality was. Here's the quote that launched a debate that had already been going for over a thousand years by Wycliffe's time:

'*For the moment, I shall naturally decline to say, concerning genera and species* [universals], *whether they subsist* [exist of themselves—are 'real'], *whether they are bare, pure isolated conceptions* [names only], *whether, if subsistent* [real], *they are corporeal or incorporeal* [physical or non-physical], *or whether they are separated from or in sensible objects* [whether universals are 'in' or 'not in' the individual physical examples], *and other related matters. This sort of problem is of the very deepest, and requires more extensive investigation.'* (Porphyry: 'Introduction') [Square brackets mine.]

Wycliffe took the view that universals—the motifs of design, classifications and genres within knowledge—originated as 'ideals' or 'arch-types' within the mind of God and emanated from Him. Hence: Wycliffe was a 'realist'. Wycliffe's opponents—William Ockham of 'Ockham's Razor' fame among them—were 'Nominalists' who took the view that universals did not have a reality beyond the literal occurrence, but were just the 'name' (hence 'nominalists') we give to the common features we abstract. You may have noticed that the dictionary definitions of 'universal', quoted at the beginning of this appendix, effectively straddle the argument.

While this may sound like a rather obscure and isolated issue, it really is the central question of spirituality, which in one form or another—theism vs. atheism; design vs. randomness; meaning vs. meaninglessness; spiritual seeing vs. spiritual blindness; consciousness is real vs. consciousness is just the name of a certain biochemical reaction—has persisted throughout the ages. For example, the Pharisees of Jesus day were realists; whereas the Sadducees—not believing in angels or the resurrection of the dead—were nominalists (though the terms come from a later era). Both camps could be wrong in various ways of course, but the Sadducees were the ones who Jesus most directly declared to be incorrect in their thinking. *'You are wrong, because you know neither the scriptures nor the power of God.'* (Matthew 22:29) To paraphrase philosophically: 'you know neither the structure nor the content of truth' or: 'you know neither universals nor their reality'. In the modern church we might say: 'you know neither the word nor the Spirit'.

I will try to avoid the many rabbit trails we could take here and throw down my own gauntlet: Jesus the 'Logos' or 'Word', who is head over all things (Ref John 1:1 and Ephesians 1:22), is the reality behind every universal within creation for in him *'...are hid all the treasures of wisdom and knowledge.'* (Colossians 2:3) And here's how I read that: The meaning of every word, the significance of every sign, the artistry behind every beauty, the order discerned in every analysis, the theory derived in every science, and every other thing about which anything can be said or thought—i.e., the whole of creation and its ongoing evolution—flows from the mind of Jesus; and therefore in his mind, the full depths and breadths and heights of it are hidden. He is the ultimate reality behind and within 'every universal' or 'all knowledge'; He is the Logos (Word). This is Jesus' original place of headship at the foundation of the world.

*'In the beginning was the Word, and the Word was with God and the Word was God. He was in the beginning with God; all things were made through him, and without him was not made anything that was made.'*
(John 1:1-3)

*'He [Jesus] is the image of the invisible God, the first born of all creation; for in him all things were created, in heaven and on earth, visible and invisible, whether thrones or dominions or principalities or authorities—all things were created through him and for him. He is before all things and in him all things hold together.'*
(Colossians 1:15-17)

To tie this in with what I have written previously, and to understand why this debate on universals is far from easy to unravel, despite the seeming obviousness from the statement about Christ being the head, we need to see our world as a battlefield in flux. Christ's headship was partially (the bit delegated to man) lost in the fall of man; but through his death, resurrection and ascension, He is restored to all authority, and given the name above every name.

However, He is not yet, in practice, fully the head of all things– there are many things not yet brought back under his headship. His authority and right is beyond doubt, but the actual enforcement has not yet happened in every corner of the universe. There are still some 'regions' in rebellion and some 'desolate wildernesses' where his authority has not yet been brought to bear. *'Now in putting everything in subjection to him, he has left nothing outside his control. As it is, we do not yet see everything in subjection to him.'* (Hebrews 2:8)

Perhaps we could compare this to a man who buys a house. He becomes the head over the whole house when he pays for it, but it may take him some time to actually make every room just as he wants to have it; for his headship to be actually established in every room. Perhaps there is redecorating required, vermin under the floor boards, and leaks in the roof... after all, this house has had squatters for a while, and stragglers may still lurk in the aft rooms.

Part of the original headship, which had been delegated to Adam and Eve and lost when they fell, was usurped by the serpent (Lucifer: probably a fallen arch angel). A squatter of course rarely ever uses the whole house or looks after it properly. In the case of creation, Lucifer was never capable of managing the whole world, and besides that, God's rearguard and mitigating action appears to resemble that of the Russians burning their assets before an advancing Napoleon: the creation was 'subjected to meaninglessness' or 'futility' as Paul says in Romans 8:20.

Nevertheless, it is evident that the serpent had control of some areas, and the Bible calls him the 'prince of this world' or 'the ruler of this present darkness' and similar things. This means that in fact the nominalists are sometimes—sort of—correct; some universals are seemingly without reality; they are just the name of an empty dwelling; the connection to the head is gone; the 'angel' or 'reality' is gone, either by its own rebellion or by God's subsequent redeployment.

I do not think any universals become absolutely unreal or totally meaningless though. They always retain at least an echo, a lingering memory of what once was and the promise of what will be again. Even the desert brings forth a cactus or two, and dry watercourses utter their remorseless croak: 'Water once flowed here.'

We are told in Jude verse 6: *'The angels that did not keep their own position but left their proper dwelling have been kept by him in eternal chains in the nether gloom until the judgement of the great day...'* This then is the context of our warfare. Some dwellings are empty and need to be filled with meaning again; some dwellings are wrongly occupied by fallen angels or demons and need to be cleared out and brought back into connection with Christ the head—and therefore presumably reoccupied by his loyal angels. Ultimately of course the realists are right—and will be 'more right'—because everything will be restored in the end. *'For the creation waits with eager longing for the revealing of the sons of God; for the creation was subjected to futility, not of its own will but by the will of him who subjected it in hope; because the creation itself will be set free from its bondage to decay and obtain the glorious liberty of the sons of God.'* (Romans 8:19-21)

In those universals wrongly occupied, we may discern a pseudo reality; false religion, occult and animism, for example. It is quite foolish to think that there is nothing behind spiritualism and the occult—there actually are spiritual beings present and active in these teachings and practices. Indeed I would go so far as to say that any group of people adhering to a teaching or practice—from train-spotters to terrorists, atheist humanists to charismatic Christians—would never come together or stay together if not for the invisible realities occupying the universals that comprise their identity. Ironically, even the 'nominalist camp' itself has an identity made up of a complex set of universals occupied by spiritual 'reality' (one of the fallen angels, Wycliffe and I would say) which may of course move on to 'greener pastures', or 'fly south' and back again, as the philosophical fashions ebb and flow across the centuries.

As far as the church is concerned, we can see in the early chapters of Revelation that the identity of each congregation, symbolically a lampstand, was no mere 'name' but in fact the 'angel of the church'. *'As for the mystery of the seven stars which you saw in my right hand, and the seven golden lampstands, the seven stars are the angels of the seven churches and the seven lampstands are the seven churches.'* (Revelation 1:20)

Perhaps in sum we could say that a true church is a lampstand alight with an angel connecting it to the head, which is Christ; whereas a light-less 'church' is a lampstand in name only; an unoccupied set of universals and the delight of the nominalist (which in this context could be another name for a hypocrite), but utterly boring to the poor reality seekers within its dreary precincts.

In a later verse, Christ warns that such a church would have its lampstand removed unless it repented. (Ref: Revelation 2:5) This parallels God's action when he subjected creation to meaninglessness. The visible consequence of this action is that an unrepentant church will fail and its members scatter, unless its 'leaders' can get hold of some false teaching and practice along with the attendant fallen angel to fill the void and hold it all together. Sound like some of church history? I'm afraid so.

But, as I said earlier, to try to penetrate this spiritual warfare paradigm with pure philosophy is a doubtful enterprise. This is because the operators—the angels and fallen angels—are probably more clever than us, certainly more knowledgeable, and in the case of the latter, exponentially more deceptive and manipulative. The serpent, for example—being master liar and hypocrite par excellence—delights in occupying the complex set of universals that comprise the identity of a group adhering to clever teachings that preclude his own existence. What better place to hide? What more comfortable place could a liar live? But of course he has other agendas and other houses too.

## Understanding Universals

I realise that this talk of universals can seem very remote, obscure, and, with my additions, weirdly mystical. So let's go back to some basics and try to get our heads around what we are actually talking about. The problem with understanding universals is not that they are so remote and obscure, but rather that they are so close and familiar; so intrinsic to language, meaning and everything that meaning relates to. We'll be using universals continually in our discussion and therefore must concentrate to narrow our focus to avoid mixing the universals we are describing with the ones we are using—but of course we are bound to be tempted by irony, humour and various other literary subtleties that involve the interplay of universals slightly out of category—paralleled, implied... and multiple other twists. Let's start with the basics.

Professor Paul V. Spade, who wrote the introduction to Kenny's translation of Wycliffe's *On Universals*, takes the simple example of the black ink in his pen—'blackness' being the universal which exists in multiple individual instances; i.e., every black thing. The reality question concerns whether blackness exists as something 'real' apart from the individual instances; i.e., is there such a thing as 'blackness'? Is blackness an 'idea' in 'heaven'? Is it an arch-type in the mind of God? Is there a 'spirit' of blackness? In Plato's terms: does the very form of blackness exist; 'blackness of itself, by itself'? The realists would answer yes to one or more of those questions. The nominalist would say 'blackness' is just the name we give to what we see before us when we look at black things.

But of course the argument is never as simple as that because every term we use has baggage—acknowledged or otherwise. Even the word 'name' itself carries a world of 'ideas' and 'spiritual elements' of one kind and another, enabling the nominalist to smuggle in some spiritual reality without admitting it. If we say 'blackness', the human mind immediately latches on to the universal and makes the connection, not just with two black pens but multiple other blacknesses—from the proverbial hat to the lowly tyre; from dark night to endless void; deepest coal mine to 'stygian cave forlorn'... unreal? It could hardly be less real than the human spirit that engages it. If the nominalist position was actually true, there would be no one remotely interested in discussing it; each 'blackness' would remain unconnected and irrelevant. But of course that can't really be imagined... or, should I say 'unimagined'?

In one of the chapters above, I talked about 'redness' coming into fashion for a while in response to prayer in the Holy Spirit. In that case I had a sense of redness swirling around in my imagination and in the air around me—I could almost feel and taste it. I understood it as an impression and essence brought directly to my spirit by the Holy Spirit who is also called the 'Spirit of truth' or the 'Spirit of reality'.

A seemingly less mystical example of simple colour universals having reality is found in the corporate world and a case of 'ambush advertising'. Here's how it happened. Thirty-six pretty, blue-eyed blonde women in orange mini-dresses appeared at a World Cup football match in South Africa (2010), sat on the front row and were having a great time until... they were forcibly removed by the security forces.

'In the second half, about forty stewards surrounded us and forced us to leave the stadium. They pushed us up the stairs, and one of the girls fell. The police came over and kept asking us the same questions over and over again... girls were crying. It was bad,' said Barbara Castelein, one of the thirty-six.

Why all this unpleasantness? Was it because they had

no tickets? No; they all had properly paid front-row tickets. Was it because they were blonde? No; there are no laws against blonde girls going to football matches in South Africa. Aha—it was because they were blowing those annoying vuvuzela horns! No! Those horrid things—more's the pity—were legal. Well then... was it because... the dresses were too short? No; the police and security men didn't have a problem with short dresses at all.

It was actually because the officials of FIFA (the governing body for international football) believed that a sinister reality called 'the corporate identity of Bavaria Brewers' occupied the simple universal 'orangeness' that day. The blonde girls nobly defended the nominalist position: that the 'orangeness' of each dress was unrelated to the other dresses and that there was no outside reality behind them each being present on the front row. 'The colour of the dresses just has the same *name* as Bavaria's corporate colour,' one of the girls might have said, with the sweetest blondeness a policeman had ever heard, or any nominalist had ever uttered.

But in the end—despite the mystical allure of lashes fluttering over blue eyes and blondness swirling between head and heart—the police were unconvinced. They doubted the likelihood of such a large coincidence and strongly suspected those clever connivers at Bavaria's advertising department. According to the *Daily Telegraph*, a police source said, 'It looked quite premeditated—someone paid them money, bought their tickets and sent them in there.' (Only one of the girls would have known for sure about the 'reality inhering'—i.e., actual personalities: planning, willing, and paying—within and behind the 'orangeness' that day.)

Bavaria's spokesman made the observation that 'people should wear what they want' and 'FIFA don't have a monopoly over orange'; but even that vague nominalism and glint of Ockham's razor (the principle that the simplest explanation should be preferred, as put forward by Wycliffe's old adversary, William of Ockham) did not assuage the wrath of FIFA against the company that had not paid for any advertising at the event.

The Dutch foreign minister also pretended to be a nominalist, suggesting that the treatment of the girls was 'inappropriately harsh for just wearing an orange dress'. I would say being a nominalist is the same as hypocrisy in the first place—but to just pretend to be a nominalist because it would be politically helpful for nominalism to be true... well, that's taking hypocrisy to an entirely new level. Trust a politician!

And of course this wasn't the first time the Dutch got into trouble. Four years earlier, in Germany, large numbers of Dutch fans had arrived in orange lederhosen (Bavaria Brewers again). When forbidden access in their trousers, they simply removed them and walked in anyway. This time the 'orangeness' made its reality known in absentia. Like the croaking parched watercourse I mentioned earlier; the knickers and underpants proclaimed in chorus: 'Orangeness was here.' (As to what the heavy-minded, bearded, and black-caped and capped creatures of Wycliffe's era would have made of these 'goings on', I truthfully cannot say!)

## The Human Body

The human body, being itself a complex set of universals, provides the ideal example to consider the question of reality. When a human body is also inhabited by a human spirit, we say it's alive; the universals have reality. If the universals of the body are altered much—say by a sword or bullet or disease—the spirit is forced to abandon it; it becomes an unfit dwelling place. We call that death; and wisdom notes that the spirit's tenure is in fact quite fragile. The apostles referred to their physical bodies as a 'tent' or 'clothing'; a temporary and soon-to-be-put-off dwelling place. (Ref: 2 Corinthians 5:1, 4; 2 Peter 1:14)

Since the living human body, like the whole realm of angels and demons, is in constant flux, static philosophical frameworks can be very misleading; we must engage dynamically if we are ever to approach truth. With the human body, static study is like dissecting a cadaver; dynamic study, like having a cup of tea with a person. The nominalist is happy (so he claims!) to name all the bits of the cadaver, right down to mapping the human genome (glory and honour to 'science'!); the realist enjoys a relationship with the 'reality' that occupies the complex set of universals called the human body: a person! Why, they might even fall in love, get married and have a baby; mixing their universals together... Mum's eyes and Dad's nose and Grandpa's funny ear... Of course nominalists can do all that too—they just don't have a clue what's going on. In fact, even those extreme nominalists who are called atheists are able to live well beyond their means (so to speak) and can enjoy God's blessings and 'the grace of life' because God is so 'gentle and lowly of heart' that He 'sends rain on the just and the unjust'—nor has He any pleasure in proving people wrong; and still less, in forcing them to agree with Him. (Ref: I Peter 3:7; Matthew 11:9; 5:45)

## LEVELS OF REALITY

Between the nominalist and the realist positions on universals, as I have already suggested, there may appear to be grounds that could support either view. This has been caused by disorder and rebellion within the spiritual realm, human complicity beginning with the fall in Eden, and of course God's action in response to it all. With my 'mystical theory of universals' (as my friend Tamsin—who, though not yet as famous as Kenny or Wycliffe, also studied philosophy at Oxford—calls it) involving as it does the Holy Spirit, angels, demons and also the human spirit in the human body, an absurdity may seem to arise in considering varying degrees of reality. Surely a person is either present or absent, not partially present.

Not so! The Bible speaks of the Holy Spirit as a person but also uses metaphors such as water and fire which can vary in quantity and levels of intensity. Even in the ministry of Jesus the gospel writers seemingly noted times of greater power and presence of the Holy Spirit. (e.g., Luke 5:17 *'...and the power of the Lord was with him to heal.'*) Certainly in our own experience and in church history, there have been times of greater and lesser intensity of Holy Spirit anointing and presence. Even in our closest-to-hand example—our personality inhabiting our body—there are degrees of presence or reality. We might even say such things to each other as, 'You're not yourself today.' Studies have shown that personality can alter with excessive stress, and then of course sickness and accident such as brain damage and Alzheimer's disease can cause varying degrees of loss right down to the extreme of a coma—where we may be unsure if the person is still there or not. In less extreme situations of dementia, the original personality may seem to fade in and out. This of course is very troubling and distressing to friends and family but it does give us some insight into the interface between spirit and body; the spiritual and the physical.

As with the level of presence of the Holy Spirit and the human spirit, the reality level in universals generally comes in varying degrees. Let's go back to 'orangeness'. In the example of the thirty-six blonde girls in orange dresses at the football match, it was very clear to FIFA, the police and everyone else that the reality of the 'orangeness' was in fact the corporate identity of Bavaria Brewers. If that had not been the case, Bavaria would not have bothered to spend money hiring the agency that sent the girls to the match. As it was, Bavaria created a strong corporate identity and presence in the arena without paying a penny to FIFA. Even so, the totality of that identity was not present, nor was it everywhere in the arena—if there had been three hundred and sixty girls in orange dresses, it would have been stronger and so on. The policeman spokesman's comment, 'It looked quite premeditated...' indicates a variable degree in the reality level. The police detective discerns a culprit behind the clues... but would a jury believe it... and just think what the barrister would do with these so-called 'facts'. Perhaps he would mention the baby with orange juice in a bottle, the man eating an orange, or the three ladies from Saskatchewan with tiger lilies on their hats.

The policeman's 'looked quite premeditated' might 'look quite lame' after that. Amidst ridicule and raucous laughter, the nominalists might win the day... but of course we would all still know they were wrong: Bavaria *was* behind those thirty-six blonde girls in orange dresses, and in the end FIFA and Bavaria and the girls (all realists after all) made a private out-of-court settlement. We all make comments similar to the policeman's about numerous things all the time as we judge degrees of meaning, authority, clarity, and 'presence' in the universals we constantly observe. Of course police detectives could never be nominalists; one has to believe real culprits are behind clues in order to solve crimes.

And companies are very concerned about the 'strength' of their corporate identity or 'brand'. (Poor old Budweiser, the official sponsor at the 2010 World Cup, with its fully paid 'redness' and 'blueness' being upstaged by 'orangeness' again, might have been looking for a little discount from FIFA—which may help us discern the reality behind all those universals of 'angriness' we were observing.) Of course strength of branding concerns not just advertising but also such things as the management of departments, divisions, franchises and the overall public image of the company.

We conclude, then, that within such things as colours and all the other universals or motifs of corporate branding, various levels of strength or presence, far from being philosophically absurd, are in fact the bread-and-butter, day-to-day work of graphic artists, designers, advertising agents, managers and others. And of course all this bread-and-butter work, in another context, is called spiritual warfare. Which is why our discussion of reality levels in universals is not only perfectly reasonable but also highly relevant to the themes of this book—and for that matter, to every element of life, from baking cakes to running for President.

In any universal or set of universals, the reality level can be altered. The atmosphere in a house can be changed by a good clean; even more by redecorating. The atmosphere and morale in a workplace can be changed for better or worse in hundreds of different ways—a field of study in itself. The atmosphere of any gathering of people can also be changed, whether it's a club, a party, a social occasion, a family meal, a class or a church meeting. In any of these situations we have an instinctive and learned knowledge of how the atmosphere may be changed for better or worse. Of course prayer of various kinds is crucial in this; indeed, it was in prayer that the first church asked for and received the Holy Spirit—the spirit of truth or 'reality'—into and upon themselves individually and corporately: the Spirit of Christ, inhabiting the body of Christ.

## The Interface of Spirit and Body

Whether we are talking about the reality in simple universals like colour, or more complex sets of universals like the human body or a group of people with some common cohesive beliefs and practices, there is difficulty in explaining how the 'reality' or 'spirit' actually interfaces or relates to the physical or individual instances of the universal. How did the corporate identity of Bavaria Breweries connect to the thirty-six girls in orange dresses? How does the human consciousness or mind connect or interface with the physical brain? How does the religious spirit dwell in a group of hypocrites? How does the Holy Spirit inhabit the true church? How does any reality connect, interface or inhere in any universal?

The reality vs. nominalism debate in all its forms often flounders in this question. The problem for the nominalists and atheists and materialists in general is that they do not want to believe that any separate thing beyond material—i.e., 'spirit' or 'mind' or 'personality' or 'consciousness'—exists, because once they do, it becomes obvious that there is a God, and even more pointedly, that he may have a moral demand upon them. All the rest of the hot air on this topic is really the sleight-of-hand distractions and machinations of deceptive magicians. Or, even if sincere, at least deceived, like those builders of perpetual motion machines that somehow lose the truth of the conservation of energy in bewildering—but irrelevant—complexities. For me, human mind and consciousness are givens before the discussion starts... otherwise there is no discussion. Long ago I gave up on solving the folly of every perpetual motion machine or unravelling every error in logic. Life is too short for that.

However, even for realists, it is hard to understand the connection and interplay between universals in knowledge and the realities that—at least potentially—inhabit them. Indeed, even for mystics who regularly discern and engage this realm, perhaps some explanations could be helpful. But of course this is the subject of a whole book, or even many books, so we will be necessarily very brief, and once again avoid the myriad rabbit trails and caveats that have plagued this discussion.

At the simplest level, universals are 'words' where the reality is the 'meaning', or 'definition' of that word. A person who stops at this level is sometimes called a 'conceptualist'—halfway between nominalism and realism. But surely we all know that there is more to words than the definition. Are there not such things as: 'anointing', 'authority', 'clarity', or 'effectiveness' of a word? Admittedly, these factors are highly variable—more art than science, and more spirit than material. But to say they don't exist at all is still nonsense that no one actually believes.

The degree to which any word 'works'—or has these 'artistic' or 'spiritual' elements—depends not only on what it contains but on what its source *intended* it to contain and what its recipient *perceives* it to contain. And that is just the sort of thing that materialists and nominalists don't even want to consider possible—because it's so difficult to quantify—but of course it is the normal stuff of relationships that we all work with every day, and all believe in, whether we want to admit it or not.

The reality of Bavaria's identity dwelling in the thirty-six girls in orange dresses was dependant on the observers recognising the 'language' of the source and knowing what it meant—if someone knew nothing of Bavaria beer, they would not have recognised that thirty-six girls in orange dresses meant anything (probably large numbers didn't). So the meaning or 'spiritual reality' was dependant on source and recipient entering into 'conversation' with the 'spirit' or 'meaning' existing between them; but exactly how it relates, inhabits or inheres in detail like the 'orangeness' is very hard to exactly pin down—though not actually any harder than in an ordinary conversation.

Similarly we could discuss how meaning inhabits or inheres within words written on paper or sound waves in the case of spoken words. Both of these are dependent on additional knowledge in both the speaker or writer and the listener or reader. Language is an extension of the thoughts of one personality to another personality, but must be recognised as such if connection between the two (conversation) is to take place. All expression (language, art, music, etc.), which is the same as saying every universal, is an extension from one personality to another... though if we don't understand the 'language' or even recognise it as a language, we may not be aware of that personality.

C. S. Lewis, in his essay *'Transposition'*, takes the example of a dog, to whom 'a finger pointing at food' is just 'a finger'; the dog sniffs at the finger rather than looking at the food the finger is pointing at. The meaning of a finger pointing doesn't exactly inhabit the finger— no dissection or analysis of the finger will find additional substance. But meaning does nevertheless exist in the whole paradigm of someone pointing and someone understanding. If we have a dog-like mind that can't 'read' a sign, we will never connect with the meaning and might even become materialists and nominalists. Jesus rebuked the Pharisees for this inability to read the signs, because the human mind is capable of 'reading', and any claim to 'doggy ignorance' is highly suspect. It is likely even to be evidence of prejudice and hypocrisy.

The Bible links the meaning or anointing in words to breath: all scripture is 'God-breathed.' (Ref: 2 Timothy 3:16) This connection between spirit and breath is made from the beginning of scripture: the spirit is actually called the 'breath' or 'wind' in Genesis chapter one.

Perhaps we could say that the *spirit* or *reality* of a word, in any form (written, spoken, acted out, etc), accompanies that word just as the breath accompanies a spoken word.

The Psalmist grapples with universals and reality, or word and meaning, and the interface mystery poetically: *'The heavens are telling the glory of God; and the firmament proclaims his handiwork. Day to day pours forth speech, and night to night declares knowledge. There is no speech, nor are there words; their voice is not heard; yet their voice goes out through all the earth, and their words to the end of the world.' (Psalm 19:1-4)*

Our problem in pinning down the interface is that we are hard-pressed to define spirit and personality: the link, in this example, between what the heavens are saying and the person of God; the 'language' of the heavens. We will fail to understand what spirit is, and how personality is extended in variable degrees within communication if we look only in the material realm. Consciousness, personality, spirit, or whatever we wish to call it, obviously interfaces with the physical realm in our bodies but we only recognise it by communication. Every message carries something of its source personality within it, just as every speaker releases breath. In this metaphor, the materialist is like a man who believes only in solids and refuses to acknowledge the gaseous. Perhaps one day someone will invent something like *Star Trek*'s 'multiphasic scanner' that will be able to detect 'spirit' and transpose its readings into measurable quantities—but I won't be holding my breath on that one. And actually, we already have something better: the human spirit restored and bonded to the Holy Spirit is able to discern with the mind of Christ himself.

And even fallen man is able to recognise and operate in spiritual realities far beyond what he fully understands, or in some cases, admits. An artist is able to put something of 'himself' into his work which continues even after he is gone; likewise a musician or writer or any other creative expression. Whether words, music, art or any other form of communication, we all know that there is a person behind it; just as we knew there was a person or persons behind the thirty-six girls in orange dresses: *someone* was trying to *say* something. Personality or consciousness is primary to any material; it is before any communication and is also the faculty by which we recognise communication. All of us human beings, whatever we claim to believe, actually operate from this assumption and do not know—nor can we imagine—a world that is otherwise.

## UNIVERSALS AND CREATION

The difficulty with getting your head around universals arises not because they are rare and obscure but because they are in fact everything everywhere. Perhaps the truest thing that can be said about universals is that they are the opposite of 'nothing'. And nothing is a far cry from the 'empty space' and all the other 'nothings' that the word 'nothing' inclines us to imagine. Our minds go to work on all the universals of all the 'nothings', including their realities, the moment we hear the word *nothing*! The empty cupboard; the empty tomb; the after-party feeling; the fruitless day; the forty-seven dresses and outfits that don't feel just right for the occasion, are all part of the rich heritage named 'nothing'. But, true, 'nothing' is that to which no thought or word applies—so we can't even use the word 'nothing'. Someone has said, '"Nothing" is what rocks dream about.' I suspect even that may be saying too much.

This 'unnameable nothing', apart from the mind of the creator himself, is precisely where the Bible begins the story of creation. Two little words are used: 'Tohu' and 'Bohu'; 'formless' and 'void' respectively. Formless means there were no universals, and void means there were no realities to inhabit any universals. There were no dwelling places and no inhabitants; no words and no definitions; no art and no meaning; no voice and no breath (spirit); truly nothing. Except of course the spirit moving in the depths of God's mind, forming the words that were about to be spoken. The Bible's opening picture, the Spirit moving upon the face of the deep, is a picture of the inner consciousness of God: his mind or personality. From that place, every universal and every inhabiting reality sprang into being; all that exists came from the word and breath that proceeded from the mouth of God.

And this, as I read him, agrees with Wycliffe's understanding that universals originate in the mind of God. The reality is the meaning that God had in his mind in the beginning, drawn from the depths and released through his spirit, which proceeded from him, as breath proceeds from a physical body. This is not as mysterious and speculative as it may first seem. An artist paints from ideas in his mind and if he is successful we sense his spirit or presence in the painting when we view it. The painting is a 'spirit to spirit' or 'personality to personality' communication link and something of the essence (another word for 'spirit') of the artist's personality must be 'in' the painting. We are not talking pantheism here; the artist's consciousness remains in his body, but something—'spirit' or 'presence'—from his personality is also in the painting. Similarly the creation was imbued with the presence of God but his personality remained in heaven and later came to walk with man in the garden in the cool of the day; just as an architect may build a house to his precise taste and delight—putting himself 'into it' we might even say—and then walk around its rooms and enjoy it.

However, as we have already been discussing, this connection or 'presence' has been far from straightforward since the fall of man. Even still, to suggest that any universal could exist without a mind being its source—whatever the reality level—is utterly and intrinsically foolish by definition. Universals and their contents, like words and meaning, are by definition the 'stuff' that proceeds from personality. Apart from the person of God and the universals that have come from him, there is only absolute nothing... minus that name, 'nothing'.

The so-called science that wants to suggest the big bang occurred when matter and anti-matter split apart and eventually evolved into all we observe to exist, may not violate the laws of conservation of energy mathematically, but philosophically it is the same old cheat that nominalists have been trying to deceive us with for centuries. Philosophically, their statement of existence goes like this: Nothing divided in half into something and anti-something... well, actually: everything and anti-everything.

However, even if we allow, mathematically in terms of matter and energy, that everything plus anti-everything equals nothing, philosophically this 'thing' the nominalist has named 'nothing' is an awful big and complicated 'nothing'. As if it wasn't enough to smuggle the whole universe into that little name, 'nothing', they've brought in the whole anti-universe as well. Philosophically—in terms of mind and knowledge and personality and meaning and universals—this is a lot more than any rock could dream up. In terms of universals (meaning, design, etc.), everything plus anti-everything is not equal to nothing, but actually two times everything. Even the most die-hard nominalist has to admit that, whatever the arithmetic, he still has two names ('universe' and 'anti-universe') in his head; and whatever the anti-universe may be, only a fool would suggest that the universe is not, in fact, quite an elaborate 'thing'.

Besides all that, we haven't yet asked what volition could have driven this symmetrical and pregnant 'nothing' to split and evolve as it evidently has... I think I might even allow Ockham's Razor on this one!

Vance Royal Olson

## On Quantum Theory

There is one other aspect of science that I may as well mention here, and that is quantum uncertainty. For some wishful nominalists, this has become the magic rabbit from the science hat, to gloss over the obvious follies of materialism. Even more wishful would be a hint that quantum theory supports personality or consciousness arising from biochemical reactions; matter over mind, so to speak. Indeed—though obviously this short section does not pretend to cover the subject comprehensively—the reverse seems like better science to me. The enigma of quantum mechanics suggests that the observer—that is, the person watching, thinking and deciding—affects the properties of the sub-atomic particle, not that the particle affects the observer; so, more like mind over matter, than matter over mind.

This effect by the observer is partly why quantum theory is so counterintuitive; the observable universe is not usually directly changed by our thinking (unless we are Jedi knights or have magical powers), whereas the sub-atomic realm apparently is.

Of course the mind and body we each have is similarly counterintuitive—or would be if we weren't so used to it—and also fits with the idea of mind controlling matter. Our bodies move, and our mouths speak, as directed by our minds. Consciousness is always cause, never effect. Indeed, Schrödinger's equation (a key quantum theory equation) may begin to define that mysterious interface of spirit and body, ultimately pointing to the great 'Logos' or 'mind of Christ' behind the universe. Quantum theory, therefore, offers no support to a notion that consciousness could arise from bio-chemistry; rather—if relevant to the discussion at all—that bio-chemistry arose from consciousness.

## Appendix 2

# The Armour of Ghostly Battle

When I was researching Wycliffe's philosophy at the old reading room of the British Library, one small book I found and enjoyed contained a selection of Wycliffe's sermons in English. The most memorable and enticing sermon had the title *The Armour of Ghostly Battle*. It was based, as you would expect, on Ephesians Chapter 6, but it had an interesting medieval twist: he likened our physical body to a knight's horse, not to be treated cruelly or harshly but made to serve us, as we in turn served the Lord. Sometimes monks and so-called holy men have taken the mortification or harsh treatment of the body as a path to spirituality. Buddhism was founded in this way, and this wrong thinking may be one of the roots of false spirituality in medieval monasticism that Wycliffe was correcting.

This kind of asceticism is still an ever-present danger to all of us; indeed, it's one of the religious spirit's favourite tricks. If the enemy can't ensnare by indulgence, he tries to lure us into prideful, self-inflicted suffering; excessive fasting, lack of sleep, overworking, and other abuses of the body. *'These have indeed an appearance of wisdom in promoting rigor of devotion and self-abasement and severity to the body, but they are of no value in checking the indulgence of the flesh.'* (Colossians 2:3)

So... be kind to your 'horse'... but make it obey!

*Vance Royal Olson*

## *The Armour of Heaven, or of Ghostly Battle*

Almighty God saith by holy Job, that all man's life upon earth is fighting, that is battle against spiritual enemies and sin. St. Paul saith: Clothe yourselves in the armour of God that ye may stiffly stand against temptations and deceits of the fiend. Man's body is as a cloth with which his soul is hid; and as a horse that bears his master through many perils. And to this horse, that is, man's body, belong many things, if he will bear his master aright out of perils. For no knight can securely fight against his enemy, unless his horse be obedient to him; no more can the soul fight against the wiles of the fiend, if the flesh, which is his horse, live in lusts and likings at his own will.

For holy writ saith: He that nourisheth his servant, that is, his body, delicately or lustfully, shall find him rebel when he least expecteth. As soon as man begins to live wisely, and flees divers lusts and likings, and vanities, which he before used and loved, and bows himself under the yoke of God's holy doctrine, then his enemies begin to contrive by wiles, frauds, and temptations, to make him fall. And therefore it is needful that his horse be meek, and helping his master to overcome his enemies. For if the soul and the body be well agreed together, and either of them helps the other in this spiritual contest, the fiend shall soon flee and be overcome. For Holy Scripture saith, Withstand ye the fiend, and he shall flee from you.

But it were great folly for any man to fight upon an unbridled horse, and if the horse be wild and ill taught, the bridle must be heavy, and the bit sharp, to hold him again. And if the horse be easy and obedient to his master, his bridle shall be light and smooth also. This bridle is called abstinence, with which the flesh shall be restrained, that he have not all his will, for he is wild and wilful, and loth to bow to goodness. With this bridle his master shall restrain him, to be meek and bow to his will. For if he will fight without a bridle upon him, it is impossible but that he fall. But this bridle of abstinence should be led by wisdom, so that nature be holden by strength, and the wildness of the flesh be restrained by this bridle. For else his horse will fail at the greatest need, and harm his master, and make him lose his victory.

This bridle must have two strong reins, by which thou mayest direct thy horse at thy will; also they must be even, and neither pass the other in length. For, if thou drawest one faster than the other, thy horse will glide aside, and go out of his way. Therefore, if thy horse shall hold the even way, it behoves thee to draw the reins of thy bridle even. The one rein of thy bridle is too loose, when thou sufferest thy flesh to have his will too much, in eating and drinking, in speaking, in sleeping, in idle standing or sitting, and all other things that the flesh desires beyond measure and reason. The other rein of the bridle is held too strait when thou art too stern against thine own flesh, and withdrawest from it that which reason would that it should have. Whoso straineth either of these reins uneven, will make his horse glide aside and lose his right way. If thou sufferest thy flesh to have its full liking, he that should be thy friend becomes thy decided foe. If thou withholdest therefrom that which it ought to have to sustain its nature, as its need requires, then thou destroyest its strength and its might, so that to help thee as it should it may not. Therefore sustain thy horse that he faint not, nor fail at thy need. And withdraw from him that vain tale telling which might turn thee to folly.

Yet thy horse needs to have a saddle, to sit upon him the more steadfastly and seemly to other men's sight. This saddle is mansuetude [mildness or gentleness] or easiness. That is, whatsoever thou doest, be it done with good consideration; wisely thinking of the beginning and the ending, and what may fall thereof; and that it be done sweetly and meekly, and with mild semblance. That is, that thou mildly suffer slanders and scorns, and other harms that men do against thee, and neither grieve thyself in word nor in deed. And though thy flesh be aggrieved, keep mildness in heart, and let not any wicked words out of thy mouth or tongue, and then thou shalt be made glad. As the prophet saith: The mild and the meekly suffering shall joy forever, who do mildly, with easiness and love, whatsoever they do; that their outward and inward semblance and cheer. Be so mild and lovely in word and deed that others may be turned to good by their example. This virtue, which is called mansuetude, that is, mildness of heart and of appearance makes man gracious to God, and seemly to man's sight, as a saddle makes a horse seemly and praiseable.

Two spurs it is needful that thou have to thy horse and that they be sharp to prick thy horse if needful, that he loiter not in his way; for many horses are slow if they be not spurred. These two spurs are love and dread; which of all things most stir men to the way of heaven. The right spur is the love that God's dear children have for the lasting weal that shall never end. The left spur is dread of the pains of purgatory and of hell, which are without number, and never may be told out. With these two spurs prick thy horse if he be dull and unwilling to stir himself to good. And if the right spur of love be not sharp enough to make him go forward on his journey, prick him with the left spur of dread to rouse him.

Separate thy soul from thy body by inward thought, and send thy heart before, into that other land; and do as a man would do that of two dwelling places must choose one, into which when he had once entered he must dwell world without end. Certainly, if he were wise, he would send before some of his near friends to see what these places were. Two places are ordained for man to dwell in after this life. While he is here, he may choose, by God's mercy, which he will; but if he be once gone hence, he may not do so. For whithersoever he first cometh, whether he like it well or ill, there he must dwell for evermore. He shall never after change his dwelling, though he feel it ever so evil. Heaven and hell are these two places, and in one of them, each man must dwell. In heaven is more joy than maybe told with tongue, or thought with heart; and in hell is more pain than any man may suffer. With these two spurs awake thou thy horse, and send thy heart before, as a secret friend, to espy these dwelling places, what they are. In hell thou shalt find all that heart may hate, default of all good, plenty of all evil that may grieve any thing in body or in soul. Hot fire burning, darkness, brimstone most offensive, foul storms and tempests, greedy devils, open mouthed as raging lions, hunger and thirst that never shall be quenched there is weeping, and wailing, and gnashing of teeth, and thick darkness. Each hateth the other as the foul fiend, and ever curse the time that they wrought sin. Above all things they desire to die, and they are ever dying, and fully die they never shall, but ever dying live in pain and wo. They hated death while they lived here, but now they had rather have it than all the wide world. Souls that are there shall be dark and dim, offensive and loathsome to see. The bodies shall be heavy and charged with sin, so that they shall move neither body nor limb, but have all manner of wo that shall grieve them. They shall think upon no good, and have no knowledge but of their pains and sins that they have wrought. And of all these pains, and many more sorrows than we can tell, end shall never come.

When thou understandest that the deadly sin which man has wrought, and which is not amended with better for thinking ere he go hence, shall be bought so dearly with that everlasting pain, that thou wouldest desire rather to let thy skin be torn from thy flesh, and thy body hewn to pieces, than that thou wouldest wilfully do a deadly sin. This spur of dread shall make our horse awake, and hold him in an even way, and speed him fast forward, and cause him ever to flee deadly sin, which is thus dearly bought, and maketh man to be thus bitterly pained forever. When thy heart hath thoroughly sought all these fearful pains which the sinful shall suffer who will not leave their sins, then send him to purgatory, and look how they shall fare who shall there be cleansed. Of such as some call small sins, it is full needful to beware. For St. Augustine saith that many venial sins draw a man to perdition as one deadly sin doth. Many drops of rain make a flood and water entering little and little by the ship's bottom, and not cast out, sinketh the ship at the last, as a great wave drowns it suddenly. And since God is displeased and dishonoured by each sin, each sin is full great, though some sin is called little sin in comparison of greater sin, as St. Anselm saith.

Heretofore some that have defiled their souls with many deadly sins, and also with innumerable that are venial, oftimes for dread to offend God more, and to get forgiveness of all their sins, and to flee the pains of hell and purgatory, have forsaken all this world, and the company thereof, and have fled into desert places, to learn to love Jesus, and bewail their own sins, and other men's also. Some souls are cleansed here, and have their purgatory with fire of tribulation and persecution, meekly suffering for the truth of God, and have much trouble because they would live well. Some also are cleansed through the fire of God's love. For the love of man's soul might so fully be set on God, that God of his great grace would cleanse him in this world, so clean from each spot of sin, that after this life he should feel little or none.

And this is the right spur that should quicken thy horse to speed in his way; that thou learn to love Jesus Christ, in all thy living. And therefore send thou thy thought into that land of lite, where no disease is, of no kind; neither age nor sickness, nor any other grievance. Courtesy and wisdom there must men learn, for there all villainy is shut out. And whoso goeth thither shall there find a gracious fellowship; the orders of angels, and of all holy saints, and the Lord above them, who gladdeneth them all. There is plenty of all good, and want of all things that may grieve. There are fairness and riches, honour and joy that each man may feel; love and wisdom that ever shall last. There is no disease that men suffer here; as hypocrisy or flattery, nor falsehood, envy, and ire. Thence are banished thieves and tyrants, cruel and greedy men that pillage the poor, proud men and boasters, covetous and beguilers, slothful and licentious, all such are banished out of that pure land. For there is nothing that men may fear, but king and joy and mirth at will, melody and song of angels, bright and lasting bliss that never shall cease. Man's body there shall be brighter than the sun ever was to man's sight. — As the light of the sun suddenly flees out of the east into the west, so shall the blissful, without any travail, be where they like. And though they were sick and feeble while they lived here, they shall be so strong there, that nothing shall move against their will. They shall have such great freedom that nothing shall be contrary to their liking. The saved bodies shall never have sickness, nor anger, nor grievance. Also they shall be filled with joy in all their senses; for as a vessel that is dipped in water or other liquor, is wet within and without, above and beneath, and also all about, and no more liquor can be within it, even so shall those that are saved, be full filled with all joy and bliss. Also they shall have endless life in the sight of the Holy Trinity, and this joy shall pass all other. They shall be in full security, that they never fail of that joy, nor be put out thereof. They shall also be filled with wisdom; for they shall know all that is, and was, and shall be. They shall have full knowledge of the Holy Trinity; the might of the Father, the wisdom of the Son, and the goodness of the Holy Ghost. For in the sight of the blessed face of God, they shall know all things that may be seen of any creature. For as Augustine saith: They shall see him, both God and man, and they shall see themselves in him also. All things that are now hid from man, he shall then see and know. They shall also have perfect love to each other, for every one shall accord with the other's will. And these joys and many more than any tongue of man can fully tell, shall those have that shall be saved, both in body and soul, after the day of doom. This is the right spur, which should stir men joyfully to love Jesus Christ, and to hasten in the heavenly way. For so sweet is the bliss there, and so great withal, that whoso might taste a single drop thereof, should be so rapt in liking of God, and of heavenly joy, and he should have such a languishing to go thither, that all the joy of the world should seem pain to him. This love should move such a man to live more virtuously, and to flee sin, a hundred fold more than any dread of the pain of purgatory or of hell. For perfect love putteth out all dread, and cleanseth the soul from filth, and maketh it to see God, and to flee oft to heaven by desire, hoping to dwell there, world without end.

(An excerpt from: Wycliffe, John. *Writings of the Reverend and Learned John Wickliff*, London 1831: Printed for the Religious Tract Society by W. Clowes)